Velvet

and

STEEL

A Practical Guide for Christian Fathers and Grandfathers

John K. Ream

Resource Publications, Inc.
San Jose, California

Reprint Department
Resource Publications, Inc.
160 E. Virginia Street #290
San Jose, CA 95112-5876
1-408-286-8505 (voice)
1-408-287-8748 (fax)

Library of Congress Cataloging in Publication Data
Ream, John K., 1934-
    Velvet and steel : a practical guide for Christian fathers and grandfathers /
    John K. Ream.
            p.   cm.
        ISBN 0-89390-408-2
        1. Fathers—United States. 2. Father and child—United States.
    3. Fatherhood—Religious aspects—Christianity. 4. Grandfathers—United States.
    I. Title.
    HQ756.R385   1997
    306.874'2—dc21   97-28453

Printed in the United States of America

01 | 5 4 3

Editorial director: Nick Wagner
Prepress manager: Elizabeth J. Asborno
Production assistants: David Dunlap, Belinda Pitco
Cover design: Alan Villatuya, Mike Sagara

To Rita,
God's instrument in
my life—I love you.
To our children and
their spouses, may God
continue to bless their
efforts as parents.
To our grandchildren,
that they might bring
God to our family's
future generations.

Contents

Acknowledgments

I never visualized myself as an author. A husband, father, businessman, and teacher, yes—but not an author.

Velvet and Steel would not have been written without the encouragement of important people in my life.

Sr. Paula Hagen first saw the need and opportunity to record the lessons from scores of Effective Father Seminars. She was instrumental in convincing the people at Resource Publications, Inc., that an unpublished non-professional could have something of value to share.

Nick Wagner and Ken Guentert, with Resource Publications, Inc., have patiently led me through an unfamiliar process. Their support while I dealt with a major health problem helped me persevere to the book's completion.

My heart-felt thanks go out to my wife, Rita, and our family and friends, who are a vital part of the life stories that make up *Velvet and Steel* and help it come alive. Our children, Laura, Lisa, Kevin, and Lynda, along with their spouses, Keven, Mark, Belinda, and Jim, and our grandchildren have been my laboratory over the years. Thank you for your respect and patience as you put up with my efforts to create "quality family time."

Surely, without my wife's daily help and encouragement, I would have given up long before the job was completed. Day after day, Rita took my thoughts and phrases and lovingly turned them into sentences and paragraphs that have made *Velvet and Steel* a readable work. Her hundreds of hours of labor are proof of her love for me and for God's plan for fathers.

Finally, I acknowledge the gifts of the Holy Spirit, for without them we all are powerless.

Acknowledgments

Grateful acknowledgment is extended to the following for granting permission to reprint copyrighted materials:

From the book *Sacred Journey of the Peaceful Warrior* © 1991 by Dan Millman. Reprinted by permission of H J Kramer, P.O. Box 1082, Tiburon, CA 94920. All rights reserved.

From the book *Chicken Soup for the Soul*, by Jack Canfield and Mark V. Hansen © 1993 Health Communications, Inc. Reprinted with permission. All rights reserved.

Unless otherwise stated, all Scripture quotations are taken from *The New Jerusalem Bible* published and copyright © 1985 by Darton, Longman & Todd, Ltd. and Doubleday & Co. Inc., a division of Bantam Doubleday Dell Publishing Group, Inc. Reprinted by permission of the publishers.

Verses marked (TLB) are taken from *The Living Bible* © 1971. Used by permission of Tyndale House Publishers, Inc., Wheaton, IL 60189. All rights reserved.

Scripture quotations marked (NIV) are taken from the *Holy Bible, New International Version.*® NIV®. © 1973, 1978, 1984 by International Bible Society. Used by permission of Zondervan Publishing House. All rights reserved.

In the event that some source or copyright holder has been overlooked, please send acknowledgment requirements to the editorial director at Resource Publications, Inc.

Introduction

One winter Saturday morning in 1978, I happened to be in the car running errands. The radio was tuned to KFUO, a Lutheran station in St. Louis.

The topic on the air was parenting—specifically, the role of fathers. The guest speaker challenged listeners to total up the time they had spent with each of their children, individually, in the last week.

As I thought about it, I felt sure I must have spent at least a couple hours with each of our four children. After all, there are 168 hours in a week. Two out of 168 was certainly within the realm of possibility.

However, I could not come up with more than thirty minutes for each child. The past week should have been a good opportunity for family interaction. I had not been traveling, as I often was during that time. Had it really been only thirty minutes per child? I felt ashamed even though the speaker said that the average American dad can't seem to fit in more than ten minutes a week for his kids. Ten minutes a week. As the words sank in I realized I had spent more time in the shower than I did with each of my children.

I thought: "It isn't my fault that no one took the time to teach me how to be a good father—my own father hadn't nor my church. Was I expected to train myself?" Then I began to realize that the past didn't matter now. The important thing was the future. Our children are God's greatest gifts to my wife, Rita, and me. They deserve much more than thirty minutes a week. That morning, I made the commitment to seek help.

Unfortunately the bookstores of the '70s did not yield much for parents beyond the writings of Dr. Benjamin Spock. I could find nothing specifically for fathers.

I guess God knew that my heart was in the right place, though, because a few days later I received a phone call from a friend from Atlanta named Jim Webb. He was very excited about a book he had just finished reading, *The*

Effective Father, written by Gordon MacDonald and published by Tyndale House (1978).

I found a copy and finished reading it in two days. I was excited and encouraged. MacDonald lays out a biblically based set of principles about what God expects an effective father to be. At last I had something to work with.

I knew I wanted to be that kind of dad. Over the next several months I set about reordering my priorities. Rita and I began to overhaul our interaction with our children.

The children will testify that I did not become a godly, effective father overnight. But as I set my sails to become a more effective father, the family began to see changes.

I tried hard to find more time to be with each child. Rita and I were determined to find ways to better share our faith with the children. I wanted to be an effective role model for them. I am not the perfect father, and we are far from being the perfect family. However, with God's help, we are at least headed in the right direction.

At the time all this was taking place I was a member of a small Christian sharing group that met Saturday mornings. We would begin each session with prayer and then share about the previous week. I often talked about the impact MacDonald's book was having. One member of our group, Alice Watson, happened to be a school guidance counselor. She impressed upon me that the problems in the majority of the children she counseled could be traced directly to an absentee father—a father who either was not there physically or one who chose not to make himself available. Alice said that those children were crying for help but there was no father to answer their call. She encouraged me to put together some sort of men's group in which I could share the principles I was learning with other fathers.

Early in 1980 we held the first Effective Father Seminar at Incarnate Word Catholic Church in Chesterfield, Missouri. Thirty of us fathers met for eight Sunday mornings. For an hour and a half we discussed the principles of effective parenting. The men came together each week to share their problems and to help each other look to God for the answers.

I only had time to hold two or three seminars a year because my career as a bank executive was reaching its peak about that time. In 1984 Rita and I moved to Chicago, where I assumed the presidency of our savings and loan. Three of our four children were then out of school and married. Lynda, our youngest, stayed in St. Louis to finish college.

While in Chicago, I continued to hold Effective Father Seminars in local churches and also for Christian businessmen in "The Loop" area. The small-group discussions proved to be the highlight of the seminars. For many, it was the participants' first opportunity to share their concerns with other men who understood and truly cared. A number of those groups have continued to meet and close friendships have formed.

In 1989 we transferred again, this time to South Florida, where I continued to hold seminars. For health reasons, I retired in 1993.

I began to seriously think about what I wanted to do with the rest of my life. There were a variety of business opportunities. I also considered working within our local church. However, my first love was and is working with fathers.

Rita suggested that if I could develop the seminar into a weekend experience, I could more easily hold seminars outside our immediate area. I held the first weekend seminar in 1994. It quickly gained popularity, and I now schedule twenty to twenty-two such weekends a year.

The Effective Father Seminars have become popular because dads are realizing that there is a battle going on and their children are the spoils. Most fathers have received little or no training in parenthood. A program that helps them understand God's purpose for fathers, while providing help developing parenting skills, is well worth their time.

But even if a program contains timely, appropriate, and well-presented material, it does not usually provide lasting answers. More often than not, behavioral changes are temporary. It is the follow-up that makes the difference.

I wrote *Velvet and Steel: A Practical Guide for Fathers and Grandfathers* to encourage continued study and sharing. It is my hope that it will be used in the following ways:

- as text to be read and studied in conjunction
  with Effective Father Seminars

- as a text shared and implemented in small groups
  of fathers or grandfathers

- as source material for grandfathers to share with their adult sons

- as a guide for individual fathers and grandfathers

I heartily recommend small-group ministry for men, not only for fathering but for everything from discipleship to mentoring. The Christian community needs men to take their lights out from under the bushels and let them shine before God, their wives, their children, and the world around them.

If we, as men of God, will pull together, nothing shall be impossible. Jesus Christ began his world-changing mission with only twelve men.

May the Lord bless each of you as you seek to be the voice of Jesus to future generations—your children and grandchildren. May God give you the courage to make a difference.

1

The Crisis

Lo, I will send you Elijah, the prophet, before the day of the Lord
comes, the great and terrible day, to turn the hearts of the fathers to
their children, and the hearts of the children to their fathers, lest I
come and strike the land with doom (Ml 3:23-24).

These words from Malachi are the final words of the Old Testament
preparing the way for the New Covenant. Jesus, in the seventeenth
chapter of Matthew, tells his disciples that Elijah has indeed returned
in the person of John the Baptist—to preach *metanoia* (a change or turnaround), a time of repentance, and a return to God.

There is little doubt that we need another Elijah or John the Baptist in our
society today to turn us back to the ways of the Lord. You and I—as husbands,
fathers, and grandfathers—are being asked to shoulder that responsibility in
our own families and make that turnaround a reality.

Involved fathers help reduce crime, child poverty, teen pregnancy, school
dropouts, gangs, rebellion, and the like. However, many fathers have turned
their backs, while others have drifted away from their family responsibilities,
abandoning their most important calling.

There are two kinds of absent fathers. The first are those who want no
involvement with their children at all. The second are those who have allowed
the material world and its pressures to distract them from their commitment
to fatherhood.

The problem is attracting widespread attention. Some seventy interfaith religious
leaders, including Jews, Catholics, Protestants, and Muslims, gathered in a Washington suburb during the spring of 1996, concerned about what the declining

child-rearing involvement of fathers is doing to America. As the prophet Malachi notes, apathetic and absent fathers are striking our land with doom.

That meeting, sponsored by the National Fatherhood Initiative, offered information which was staggering in its implications. Public awareness is needed, said one speaker, to spread the word that "fathers are more than sperm banks or automatic teller machines." Speaker after speaker affirmed that fathers must play an integral part in rearing their children and that their absence, both physically and emotionally, is contributing to a wide array of social problems.

Children ... want their fathers back.

"Children," said Wade Horn, a psychologist and director of the National Fatherhood Initiative, "don't want our money; they don't want power. They want their fathers back. I caution us all that we are running out of time." Horn noted that in 1960 about seven million children lived without their fathers. Today, he said, the number is twenty-three million, *nearly forty percent of all American children*. If this trend continues, fatherlessness in American culture will soon become the norm. We fathers have responsibilities, but we ignore these at our own peril. Horn also said children are best socialized when both their mom and dad play active roles in their lives. Mothers and fathers together provide the needed complement in child-rearing.

Mothers, noted Horn, generally provide a nurturing, cautionary figure. Fathers can provide more discipline and encourage their children to take risks. "Children do best when they are reared with high levels of warmth and high levels of control," said Horn—in other words, with mom and dad working and living *together* as involved parents.

You can, however, be an involved parent figure in a child's life without being related to that child. Rita and I met Camille Brouillard, a Catholic nun, in 1989. As part of a small support group of Christians involved in various ministries, we come together twice a month to pray and share meals and our Christian walk with one another. Camille's greatest gift is compassion. She works at Children's Diagnostic and Treatment Center in South Florida. She has a caseload of eighty-five seriously ill children, about half of whom are infected with HIV.

Our group is very important to Camille because she can unload on us a small portion of the grief that she experiences almost daily. There is rarely a week that goes by that a child does not die. Most of these children live in poor, single-parent homes headed by mothers.

I offered to become a surrogate father/grandfather to one of Camille's kids. She suggested two step-brothers, originally from Haiti. The oldest, Jean, eleven years old, who was born with HIV, now has full-blown AIDS. Gerry, a year younger, is without serious health problems. When I first met them, they were shy; we were all a bit unsure of ourselves. But I began with the usual questions about family and school.

Help needs to come from an involved individual.

Their mother had died of AIDS several years ago, and their dads were not a part of their lives. The boys were living with their older sister, her boyfriend, and the couple's two young children. The boys were attending a local elementary school but they used any excuse to remain at home. They were very bright boys, but they were struggling to perform at grade level.

Jean's health appeared to be stable. He had to be very careful about catching colds, flu, or any other infection, but for the most part he was able to do activities that any eleven-year-old boy liked to do. We spent afternoons over the next eighteen months at the Science Center, the museums, movies, the zoo, swimming, and visits to my home. Their favorite activity was eating. As soon as they would get in the car, their first question was, "When are we going to eat?" Jean loves pasta and Gerry loves hamburgers. After a while, I came to understand that they would order items that provided the largest portions. Then they would eat half and ask if it was okay to take the rest home. It wasn't difficult to understand that there wasn't a lot of food at home.

While my primary goal was for us to enjoy each other's company and to provide them with a break from a rather dull day-to-day existence, I was also interested in helping them grow by developing a deeper set of transferable skills—skills that would help them get a good job later on and experience a better way of life. As a Christian, I also prayed for the opportunity to introduce them to Jesus Christ.

As the visits and the months went by, I became frustrated. I wasn't making the inroads I had hoped to make. Personal hygiene remained a problem. Their attendance at school was spotty, and although I frequently discussed Jesus Christ, that was about all I could accomplish. I was that nice "white man" who took them places, bought clothing for them, and played games with them. I'm sure their life was just a bit better because of our relationship, but I never made the progress I had hoped to make. My own bout with cancer and the boys' move fifty miles away ended the relationship.

The lessons I came away with were many:

- Children with AIDS can live for years and lead near-normal lives.

- There is no need to fear casual contact with people with AIDS.

- The gulf between the "haves" and "have-nots" is very wide and growing.

- The chance of Jean and Gerry rising above their current situation, without ongoing support and help, is slim.

- Help needs to come from an involved individual.

- Government aid, while helpful, is not the final recourse. Single mothers/guardians should be able to expect the help of mature men who are willing to put time, effort, and love into saving this generation—*one child at a time.*

Let me illustrate with a short story by Jack Canfield and Mark V. Hansen from the book *Chicken Soup for the Soul* (Health Communications, Inc., 1993):

One at a Time

A friend of ours was walking down a deserted Mexican beach at sunset. As he walked along, he began to see another man in the distance. As he drew nearer, he noticed that the local native kept leaning down, picking something up and throwing it out into the water. Time and again he kept hurling things out into the ocean.

As our friend approached even closer, he noticed that the man was picking up starfish that had been washed up on the beach and, one at a time, he was throwing them back into the water.

Our friend was puzzled. He approached the man and said, "Good evening, friend. I was wondering what you are doing."

"I'm throwing these starfish back into the ocean. You see, it's low tide right now and all of these starfish have been washed up onto the shore. If I don't throw them back into the sea, they'll die up here from lack of oxygen."

"I understand," my friend replied, " but there must be thousands of starfish on this beach. You can't possibly get to all of them. There are simply too many. And don't you realize this is probably happening on hundreds of beaches all up and down this coast? Can't you see that you can't possibly make a difference?"

The local native smiled, bent down and picked up yet another starfish, and as he threw it back into the sea, he replied, "Made a difference to that one!"

We may not be able to reach every child who needs help, but we have to start somewhere. The obvious place to begin is the church. That is where we should look first to find the men needed to provide inspiration, training, and support for this mentor ministry to children. We can make a difference.

Children need both a mother and a father for the best chance of reaching their potential. Where the father has abandoned his role, churches must fill the gap. There are tens of thousands of grandfathers just like me, who, if introduced to the situation and trained and supported by church communities, can make a contribution to the development of fatherless children.

A short while ago I asked our youngest daughter, Lynda, to tell me truthfully just what kind of dad I had been for her. She is thirty-one years old, a physical therapist, a wife, and a new mother. She began with the phrase, "You know, Dad, you were gone a lot." Her words came as no real surprise but they made me sad. I wished I could have started over. I wonder how many children would begin a description of their own father with similar words.

Travel was a large part of my career from the time our four children were pre-schoolers until the oldest children were married and had left home. For almost twenty years I spent close to three weeks a month on the road. I was home each weekend but was busy with errands.

How did I start down that road, a road that I found nearly impossible to leave? It began with the birth of our first child, Laura. In 1957, after we had been married only a year, I accepted a transfer from St. Louis to Houston. I was a twenty-five-year-old assistant branch manager in an auto finance company. The following year, as Rita prepared to deliver our first child, she left her job with a steamship company. For the first time in our marriage we had to live on my income alone. It wasn't easy, but we were making it.

Then Laura joined us. It was a Wednesday night in April 1959. Rita had begun labor early in the afternoon. It was now 8:30 p.m. I was nervously sitting in the waiting room (they didn't allow dads in delivery back in those days). I was watching Bat Masterson on the black-and-white TV when I heard our little girl's first cry. It was a beautiful moment. But it was also frightening; it dawned on me that I would be responsible for providing every meal, every piece of clothing, her education, and the roof over her head for the next twenty years.

What I did not realize, however, was that I was being held accountable for her moral, emotional, and spiritual development as well. No one had ever taught me how to be a father. Like many men, I moved into this new era of my life thinking that my primary goal was to provide financial security for my wife and child. I worked very hard, put in long hours, took transfers, and was blessed greatly in a material way over the years.

It wasn't until fifteen years later, after I had experienced a faith conversion through the Cursillo movement, that I woke up to the fact that my children, then pre-teens, needed me in other ways. I needed to be part of their total development: moral, spiritual, and emotional. By that time, however, I was so caught up in the corporate world that it was nearly impossible for me to make little more than small mid-course changes in my career path. I did, though, continue to look for ways to give the children more of my time, love, and attention.

At times, she needs Dad's undivided attention.

Still, fathers can come home each night and still not be a vital part of their children's development. I was speaking with a young teenage girl recently. She has a deep love and respect for her father. He is a committed Christian, participates in church activities, and is home almost every evening. Every night at bedtime he invests fifteen to twenty minutes with each of his three children, sharing their day and praying with them individually. Looks like the ideal dad. But the teenager went on to say that, in her eyes, Dad spent a great deal of time alone, working either in the garage or out in the yard. She wanted to spend even more time with him, doing nothing special, just being *with* him. Here is a *good* father, who has *good* intentions, doing a *good* job, but he is still not answering the total needs of his children. At times, she needs Dad's undivided attention.

A friend of ours, who is a Christian counselor, estimates that only *one of every twenty fathers prays with his children*. The lack of a father's influence can present us with different challenges:

1. the challenge to provide surrogate fathering models for those children whose own father has abandoned them. (This answer lies within our local church communities.)

2. the challenge to dads who are physically "gone a lot," whether due to business travel, separation, or divorce, to devote more time and attention to their children.

3. the challenge to dads who are around physically but who are not investing the time, attention, or prayerful planning that their children are crying out for.

Even the best of us dads have more to do to provide the love and support our children need. The remainder of this book will be devoted to dealing with relationships, training, standards, communication, and other practical aids which, with God's help, will enable us to be more effective in our roles as father, grandfather, or both.

Discussion Questions

1. Do you agree that we are moving toward a fatherless society, with a changing definition of "family"?

2. How can you and your church community help fatherless children, one child at a time?

3. Grandfathers, would you be willing to "adopt" a child who needs a positive male role model?

4. Do you believe that fathering is more than being a good material provider? What else are fathers called to provide?

5. How much time did you invest, one on one, with each of your children this week?

6. Are you satisfied with your performance this week? Will your children agree with you?

7. Grandfathers, how have you kept in touch with your grandchildren this week? Is there room for improvement?

2

Velvet and Steel (and Other Worthy Traits)

Early in the Effective Father Seminars, I try to make it clear that the time we spend together will center on encouraging behavioral changes in us as fathers. We are not there to advise parents how to get Billy to take out the trash or Suzy to complete her homework on time. While improvement in our children's performance and behavior can be an expected result, that change will happen because *we* as *fathers* are making ongoing improvements to our lifestyle and values. Our behavior should be like a light, growing brighter, guiding our children toward their highest potential. How? By committing to become living examples of Christianity to our family and the world around us.

Our son, Kevin, is a civil engineer. He builds hospitals. His uniform of the day, usually khakis, comes complete with heavy, steel-toed work shoes. When his son, Christopher, was still in diapers, he couldn't wait for his dad to arrive home from work. Kevin usually shed his work shoes in the laundry room as he came in and soon little Chris was imitating dad by putting on his shoes and parading around the house. Now eight years old, Chris still wants to be a builder like his Dad, the *main man* and role model in his life.

When children are young, they imitate almost everything they see their parents do. What happens, however, when those children become teenagers? Chuck Colson, noted author and speaker, says that seventy-five percent of our teenagers leave the "faith of their fathers."

Three out of four of our young people, as they go to work or off to college, stop going to church because they no longer feel the need for a faith community. When asked why, teenagers gave these top three answers, according to Colson:

1. Their parents and others in church communities do not seem to practice what they preach. The word used most often was "hypocrisy."

2. Christianity, as they have experienced it, does not appear to have the answers for Monday-morning problems.

3. There are so many conflicting messages about how to live one's life, e.g., New Age or the "new morality," that they choose to move away from all faith-centered activities.

Unless we, in partnership with our spouses, are living models of a successful, joy-filled, Christ-centered life, can we expect our children to move into independent living with a sound Christian foundation?

When I speak of a *successful, joy-filled, Christ-centered life,* I'm not implying a life without problems. As Christians, we are not excused from troubled relationships, career downsizing, medical problems, or even rebellious children. The difference for us as Christians is the strength we have emanating from our relationship with Jesus Christ.

If we are to be that Christian example (good men trying to be holy), what are the vital qualities, values, and lifestyle traits that our children must see in us?

A close friend who was visiting his grandchildren had the occasion to do a bit of grocery shopping for the family. Grandpa took his eight-year-old grandson, Peter, along with him. After securing a few items they took them to the checkout counter. The total came to something less than ten dollars and Grandpa gave the checker a ten-dollar bill. Mistakenly, the young lady at the counter gave him back change for a twenty. Grandpa looked at the change and returned the extra ten dollars to the cashier. She was more than a bit taken aback but smiled and thanked him. She went on to add that most people nowadays are usually not honest enough to return the extra change. Peter was right there taking it all in as one of his role models practiced what he preached. As the pair returned to their car, Grandpa had the golden opportunity to *drive home* the virtues of honesty and integrity.

If we are committed to proclaiming "life in union with Christ" as our family ideal, then it must become reality as we live out our lives.

How can we get away with cheating on taxes, telling white lies, using radar detectors to avoid the law, and asking our children to tell the callers whom we would rather not see that we are not at home? How can we say one thing and do another? Our actions *must* mirror what we say.

During the summer of 1996 our two oldest grandchildren, Josh, fifteen, and Jessi, thirteen, spent ten days with me visiting Washington, D.C., and Boston. I picked D.C. and Boston so I might help convey a sense of history to each of them. We visited the Smithsonian, the Holocaust Museum, the Capitol, and several other historic sights.

There is always a crowd at the Washington Monument, but I sense they are there for the climb or maybe the view from the top, which is indeed breathtaking. The Jefferson Memorial, along with the new Kennedy Memorial, are both moving experiences. But the Lincoln Memorial always brings a lump to my throat and tears to my eyes. After reading his Gettysburg Address and his Second Inaugural Speech, I looked up at his bronze

How can we say one thing and do another?

likeness and felt like crawling up and sitting on his lap. What a model of human behavior he was; what a light in a time of national darkness. Carl Sandburg best describes Lincoln as a man of "velvet and steel." He was a multifaceted statesman, an almost complete human being, a model for you and me.

The "velvet" side of Lincoln was his compassion and love. He allowed himself to cry, even in public, as he felt the brokenness of our people during that troubled time. His eyes showed a depth of feeling and sensitivity rarely found in a powerful man.

As for Lincoln's "steel" side, he steadfastly steered us through those years as we shed the sins of slavery. Lincoln, indeed, was a man of "velvet and steel."

You and I, as fathers and grandfathers, can pick up more than a few hints from a man such as Abraham Lincoln.

When I try to visualize velvet, I usually see the color purple, the color of royalty. With our wives as partners, we too are called to a royal priesthood. Peter identified you and me in his first letter, as "a chosen race, a royal priesthood, a consecrated nation, a people set apart..." (1 P 2:9). We are called to be different and not of this world, even though we must operate and live in it. We are commanded to be change agents for Jesus Christ.

Velvet also reminds me of softness—gentleness for fragile spirits. We have two beautiful granddaughters, Jessi, thirteen, and Julie, nine. Jessi is more on the aggressive side, outspoken, and a risk-taker. Julie, on the other hand, is soft-spoken, reserved, and extremely tender. Their mother, my daughter Laura, and her family visited with us recently and there were occasions when

Jessi and I locked horns. I was intent on helping her to understand that at times her words sounded harsh and abrupt. We made headway that week, but I often saw a look that told me she thought I wasn't being fair. As she and her family were leaving, I took Jessi aside, held her close, and told her how special and precious she is to me. I also told her that I would always love her, no matter what. She softened. It was one of those special times, just between us.

Our actions must mirror what we say.

During their visit, we invited our daughter and her family to join Rita and me in our morning devotions. A vital part of our morning is the time we spend together in Bible study and prayer. We take about a half hour each morning to start our day in the best possible way. As all of us sat in the den, I invited Julie to join me in Grandpa's special chair. Since I'm over six feet tall and weigh more than two hundred pounds, she and I filled the chair to capacity—and beyond. But that was the point—to hold that little girl, stroke her hair and reassure her she is loved just as she is. Isn't that what we hear at church, that God loves us just as we are? Surely if fathers and grandfathers can make unconditional love real to children when they are young, won't they stand a better chance of continuing that belief as adults?

Other qualities that come to mind as I think of velvet are: flexibility, adaptability, suppleness, and extendibility. The term "men of velvet" is a theme we can work with.

Steel has very different properties from velvet, yet both are complementary. We need both. When I think of the "steel" side of Lincoln, it brings to mind his strength and durability. I visualize him with a strong, firm grip on things and as a tempered decision-maker, qualities he exhibited upon issuing the Emancipation Proclamation. We as fathers and grandfathers can bring a similar set of qualities and values to our family environments.

How we handle a crisis, a death in the family, the loss of a job, medical challenges, or even a bad day at work, will set the example for our children's behavior. Unfortunately, damaging traits, such as a violent temper, laziness, and physical and verbal abuse, have a way of recurring down through the generations. It's up to us to break negative cycles and give our children something positive to emulate.

A couple we know well, George and Pauline, were tested by just such an issue. One of their daughters, Dolores, had recently married. Jack, the husband, had just graduated from college but was having trouble finding a decent-paying job. Dolores was still in school and although she was also working part-time they were having difficulty making ends meet. To help out, George and Pauline usually invited the young couple for Sunday dinner and also gave them food for their freezer.

One morning Dolores stopped by the house to have coffee with her mother. After a few pleasantries, Dolores asked her mom if her father had ever hit her. Surprised by the question, Pauline assured Dolores that her father had never laid a hand on her and that violence was just not acceptable in any form. Pauline then asked her daughter if she and Jack were having problems. In tears Dolores confessed that Jack, frustrated with their financial situation and his inability to provide for all their needs, had gotten violent on several occasions. Mother and daughter talked for several hours. They both wanted the marriage to succeed but were adamant that abuse in any form could not be tolerated.

When George first heard about his daughter's situation he was furious. His initial thought was to teach Jack a physical lesson. However, maturity and common sense prevailed and, after a discussion with Pauline, an off-site meeting with Jack was arranged. During the meeting George made it clear to Jack that abuse in any form, physical or verbal, was totally unacceptable. George explained that men were made physically stronger by God to provide, protect, and serve their wives and children. He went on to suggest counseling and to commit his and Pauline's total support for the young couple whenever and wherever needed. Jack revealed that he himself had suffered from an abusive father and the father in turn had been abused by Jack's grandfather. The abuse had been passed down from generation to generation. In Jack's family, anger and tantrums were often the way difficult situations were handled. When an easy answer was not readily available the process was to hurt those they loved to show how much they themselves were hurting.

I am fully aware that there are no easy answers to the tidal wave of abuse that is currently flooding our society, but we must break this chain reaction. Re-forming our men to take on the velvet and steel mentality is a key element in making such a break.

Dolores and Jack have made their marriage work. They now have several children and are active in their church. Jack has matured and has become an excellent father and a good provider. The family still has its share of problems, but they now know where the answers lie—in a family relationship with Jesus Christ.

While the qualities of velvet and steel are a solid foundation upon which to build, we need to develop other attributes that our young people can observe, experience, and work into their own characters—qualities such as honesty, respect, honor, trust, and commitment.

A story I heard some time ago, shared by a Christian speaker, described one of his family's reunions. He, along with a hundred or so other family members, gathered every few years at the old homestead for a day or two of feast and fun. The speaker and his family flew into his hometown early one morning ready for the gathering. They stopped at the local grocery store to pick up food items for that day's barbecue. After he brought his purchases to the cashier and the total was rung up, the father remembered he was short on cash. There he stood, surrounded by his family, unable to pay the bill. Sheepishly he asked the checker if she would accept a personal check drawn on an out-of-state bank.

The checker frowned but called for the manager, a longtime local resident. He took one look at the check and initialed his okay. He looked up at the father and smiled, stating that anyone with that last name was good for anything they wanted in that town.

Years of family performance had built the reputation of trust, high values, honesty, and integrity. Their name stood for something. Dad could not have written a better lesson for his children to witness. And the children would think twice before they would ever damage that reputation built on years of performance. What a legacy to pass on to his kids!

Some of my own family think I am too strict about not copying computer software, but I believe it is wrong. Recently a friend and I were examining and discussing examples of Bible software. He remarked how well he liked the software and how useful the collection was for him. He went on to offer to copy it for me. Almost at once he realized what he had said and withdrew the offer.

Sin (lowering our standards) doesn't gallop into our life—it creeps in one baby step at a time. You and I need to be ever watchful—examining how and what we think, what we say, and how we put what we believe into action. In Paul's letter to the Philippians, we read: "fill your minds with everything that is true, everything that is noble, everything that can be thought virtuous or worthy of praise" (4:8).

We will never reach perfection. Each of us is on a never-ending pilgrimage; we seek to be a little more like Jesus than we were the day before. But if we don't regularly look at ourselves, make honest evaluations, and commit to improve, we will fall short. Our children and grandchildren don't expect us to be perfect. They do, however, have the right to expect us to *try* to be men of *velvet and steel*.

Discussion Questions

1. Are there times when you say one thing but your children observe another?

2. Do you respect authority? How are your driving habits? Are you always truthful? Are you proud of your language?

3. Do you have a radar detector?

4. Would you return extra change given by mistake? What if the amount was substantial, would you correct a mistake no matter how large the amount?

5. If someone described you as a man of velvet and steel, would your wife and children agree?

6. Does your family name have solid meaning in the community?

7. Grandfathers, have you shared your family history with your grandchildren?

3

Not Me but Thee

When we look at society we can see that it operates on the basic axiom "Me first, you second." The world rationalizes this order with comments such as "I need my space"; "I deserve that BMW"; and "I have earned that skiing vacation in the Alps." In other words, life is for the here and now.

There is nothing wrong with driving a BMW, taking a vacation in the mountains, or setting aside space and time to refresh ourselves. The problem arises when we lose track of what comes first, when we forget *God's order* which is: God, family, others and then me. God's order for fathers is clearly laid out in Deuteronomy 6:4-9:

> Listen, Israel: Yahweh, our God is the one, the only Yahweh. You
> must love Yahweh your God with all your heart, with all your soul,
> with all your strength. Let the words I enjoin on you today stay in
> your heart. You shall tell them to your children, and keep on telling
> them, when you are *sitting at home*, when you are *out and about*,
> when you are *lying down* and when you are standing up; you must
> fasten them on your hand as a sign and on your forehead as a
> headband; you must write them on the doorposts of your house and
> on your gates [emphasis mine].

God's mandate, especially for fathers, is very clear. We find three distinct commands as we look closely at the words of Moses to the people of Israel.

> 1. God calls you and me into a growing love relationship with
>   him. That is expanded in the New Testament to a love
>   relationship with Jesus Christ. We are moved to love,
>   worship, adore, and place Jesus Christ at the center of our
>   lives. He is our reason for being. We are to fill our hearts
>   with his love. We are commanded to observe a different

way of life. We are to be "a people set apart, a royal priesthood" (1 P 2:9).

2. Yahweh commands us to share this relationship with our children. And he gets specific. We are to share, teach, and model God's ways while we are *sitting at home* (leisure time with the children), *out and about* (Saturday errands with the children), and *lying down* (bedtime sharing with the children). This isn't just a one-time affair. God tells us that we must share his ways with our children over and over. It is a lifetime commitment between God, our children, and us fathers.

3. Yahweh, speaking through Moses, wants us to be a light to the world (see Mt 5:14). We are to show, by all we do and say, who we are and what we stand for. We are men who have not arrived, men on a pilgrimage, *good* men trying to be *holy* in this journey of life.

Our relationship with God has top priority. Passing on that relationship to our children is a close second. You and I, fathers and grandfathers, in partnership with our wives, are the primary teachers and role models whom God looks to in order to pass on the Good News.

We will be expanding on all three commands as we go on, but for now let us focus on setting priorities. How we spend our time and money is probably a good indication of where our heart is. It could also tell us what we would be willing to die for.

Several years ago Rita and I participated in a wedding ceremony. The pastor talked about a major high-rise fire that had recently taken place. As the firefighters battled the blaze, it became apparent to the crowd gathered across the street that a couple, presumably a husband and wife, were trapped on a high balcony. Ladders were unable to reach the couple. The drama heightened as the smoke and flames got closer to them. A hush fell over the crowd of spectators as they witnessed what happened next. Tenderly, the husband embraced his wife, kissed her, picked her up, stepped over the railing, and jumped. As they fell, the crowd stood mesmerized as he positioned his body beneath hers to take the impact of the fall. He gave his life so that she might live.

Certainly a noble sacrifice. A worthy expression of love between a husband and his wife. As a reader of this book, I'm sure that you fall into that same category. A man, husband, and father who would gladly give up his life for those he loves. It goes almost without saying, doesn't it?

Yes, you and I, if confronted with a fire at home, would surely be the last one out. Our wife and kids would be safe, the dog and cat would be accounted for, and we would even go back for the hamsters and goldfish (perhaps even the wedding album, at our wife's request).

Reacting in a crisis is relatively easy. The challenge is there, the danger is present, and we are expected to preserve those who look to us for protection.

Dying to self— putting thee before me.

However, dying to self—putting thee before me—can be much more difficult day by day than putting our life on the line. Habits, routines, and commitments outside the home have subtle ways of absorbing our time, interest, and energy.

A "not me but thee" philosophy moves us to regularly take stock of our priorities and ask what really matters. The first of the Ten Commandments says, "You will have no gods other than me" (Dt 5:7). It is appropriate that we honestly look at our lives periodically. Who and what are the gods in our lives?

Early in my corporate career a mentor gave me advice on how to succeed. I, of course, had to be competent—able to manage and lead. I had to know the banking business inside and out. But there were also social skills that needed to be mastered—one was the ability to play a decent game of golf. Since I enjoyed sports I took the advice seriously.

We were living in Atlanta at the time. Our children ranged in age from three to nine. Although I was putting in close to sixty hours a week and was frequently out of town, I still found time for golf; it was important to me. I managed eighteen holes both Saturday and Sunday plus an extra nine on a pitch-and-putt course Wednesday evenings.

As I headed for the door with my golfing companions one Sunday morning, my son Kevin, who was five at the time, pulled at my pant leg and said, "Are you going to play golf again, Daddy?" I can't remember my answer; I'm sure I mumbled something. But I do remember that I played poorly that day. His piercing question was right on target. Daddy was leaving him again, going out the door to be with someone else. And he could not understand why.

As I thought about it, I could not understand why, either. That five-year-old's question rang in my heart. What was it to be—golf or Kevin? The answer was clear. I had some decisions to make about my priorities.

There is much to be said for sports. Golf teaches patience, it helps one relax after a tough work week, and, for me, with my mediocre play, it can be very humbling. But did golf warrant the investment of the better part of each weekend and a midweek evening? My children thought not. I thank God that little Kevin could be honest enough to question me. "Are you going to play golf again, Daddy?" told me that I had a decision to make. *Who* or *what* was going to take precedence in my life?

To help the men who attend Effective Father Seminars get a handle on how their family views dad's or granddad's priorities, we provide a collage of pictures showing men engaged in various activities. Some are in work situations (desk piled high, at a computer, on the phone), others are in sport settings (jogging, fishing, golfing), and still others are with the family (hugging mom, playing with the kids). We ask our dads to take the poster home that first night,

"Are you going to play golf again, Daddy?"

and, if they have the guts, to ask their children to point out which pictures remind them most of dad. Then, if the dads are really courageous, they can show the poster to their wives.

At the first session the next morning we review the results. There are a few surprises. But most dads, when honest with themselves, are already aware of what they are about. What is most revealing, however, is that even young children know where dad's heart lies. We can come up with many alibis, but actions speak louder than words. Children take note of how dad spends his time. They may not always vocalize their feelings, but the feelings are there.

Another way for each of us to get inside ourselves is to identify how we define "success."

Every man needs to see himself, and be seen by others, as successful. We need to count for something, to be a contributor, to make a difference, to be *somebody*.

Our society emphasizes winning. Being a winner—getting high grades, being at the top of the class—that's what counts. Years ago I used to enjoy listening to a weekend program on public radio hosted by Garrison Keillor. It was an hour of satire about a small Minnesota town called "Lake Woebegone." The town was a place where "all the men were successful, all the women were good-looking, and the children were all above-average." Isn't that what the world would have us strive toward—to be successful, good-looking, and above-average?

Take for example the typical social gathering where we run across new acquaintances. Upon arrival—fifteen minutes late for effect—we scan the group to identify the men who appear "successful"—those who are sure of themselves, in control, and in command. In fact, with years of experience, men can make these evaluations almost unconsciously. We tactfully gravitate toward the chosen few, making sure our first words give the right impression, the impression that we, too, have arrived. We convey that we are secure financially, we are on a fast career path, we drive the right car, we live in the right neighborhood. These are the impressions we wish to impart.

Before an hour has passed, the entire group has been rank-ordered. We have identified who we want to know better, who is interesting, and, above all, who may be able to help us move along our own path to success.

Society seems to revolve around: Who do I know? Who has the power and the wherewithal to make "good things" happen in my life? Who has the key to money, power, and position?

I've gradually come to understand that secular society's way of viewing life is often quite shallow.

Rita and I were active in Christian retreat work for many years. One of the regular follow-up activities was a weekly gathering where we could experience the ongoing fellowship of friends. We began and ended the meetings with prayer and shared our week's walk with the Lord.

One Friday evening we arrived a bit late. The first activity was to break into groups of two or three and then share our week with one another. I remember entering the hall and scanning the room. I was looking for my cronies, the "pretty people," my regulars, people like myself whom I felt comfortable with, my old friends.

Rita took off to complete a group, and I was left standing alone at the door. Then I spotted a woman sitting by herself near the back of the room. I didn't really know her, although she had been somewhat active in the group for several months. She was in her mid-thirties, single, and I thought her to be a teacher of some sort. She was looking straight at me. I can remember saying to myself, "Oh no, now I'm stuck with Mary! What can we possibly have in common?" I wasn't looking forward to the next twenty minutes, and I thought, "That'll teach me to arrive late!"

Reluctantly, I joined her. We prayed and then began to share. I found out she was a teacher at a regional school for the deaf and I perceived that she was very talented. But what struck me most was her compassion and love for the little ones.

As she continued sharing she spoke of a little boy from a nearby state whom she had taken into her home so that he might attend her school. I could see how special he was to her and how her entire life was wrapped up in service to these precious children.

I was surprised and disappointed when our time together was over. It had been both an enlightening and inspiring time for me. As I walked away I felt more than a bit ashamed of my initial reluctance to join her.

Years later, I wonder who would stand out as the most successful person in the room that evening. There were a couple of us bankers, an executive from a chemical company, an owner of a printing concern, and several from different religious communities. And then there was a shy, meek, underpaid teacher of deaf children.

When is enough enough?

Mary and I became friends after that, and partially through sharing her joy of working with special children, my family was led to take in newborn foster babies. These tiny infants brought much happiness and love to our home. Although our hearts were broken to see one leave, they soon mended with the arrival of the next baby. Those years were a special time of bonding and growth for our teenagers, especially our daughters. They developed skills and confidence which have served them well now that they have children of their own.

But even more importantly, eight infants received an abundance of love and attention, a good beginning, and a proper preparation for life with their new adoptive parents. Who would have thought all this would stem from a reluctant moment of sharing with a lovely woman one Friday evening?

My definition of success expanded that evening. Let me challenge each of you: What does success mean to you, and how are you using your God-given talents and skills to make it happen in your life? Are you looking for financial independence or to increase the size and scope of your job? There is nothing wrong with those endeavors, but true success is much, much more.

At the end of this chapter you will be given the opportunity to define or redefine what success is to you and your family. I pray that you will choose your definition carefully.

I agree that even after we have looked at our priorities and have re-examined the meaning of success, there are still bills to pay and food to put on the table. There are house payments to make and college education and retirement savings that need to be provided for. Most of us will never win a lottery or find that a rich aunt has left us financially secure. We will have to put in years of hard work to live a comfortable life. But, when is enough *enough*?

Late in my career, the business unit I was managing performed superbly. The bank as a whole also did extremely well. It had been a great year, and our people had exceeded their business goals. Bonus time came and with great expectation I awaited the all-important call from my boss, our division head.

When it came, the financial reward was even greater than I expected. For the next few days I was on "Cloud Nine." Very quickly, however, the cloud faded as I set my sights on how to obtain an even bigger bonus the next year. How could I stretch myself and those around me to perform at even higher levels?

There is nothing wrong in seeking ways to increase performance. But that year's bonus was more than we really needed. It was more than enough. Why then wasn't I satisfied? Why did I continue to push? When would *enough be enough*?

I paid a very high price for that bonus in time and energy. Even when I was at home my mind was often on business issues. My family paid an even higher price, for my heart was often elsewhere. For me, enough was rarely enough. As I look back, there are several transfers which I would now rethink, many nights when I would have left the work at the office, and business trips which I would have postponed.

A co-worker named Frank was a highly skilled financial officer. His career with the bank had taken him and his family to many foreign countries. He once shared with me about an assignment to Australia he had accepted. Since the business situation there was critical he had agreed to leave at once. His wife and nine children were left with the task of selling their home, packing their belongings, gathering school and medical records, arranging for passports, and scheduling the transportation to their new home.

Frank described the scene as he met his family at the airport. He told me that he felt more than a bit sheepish as he realized what a load he had placed upon his wife.

That transfer was just one of the many times that Frank had placed career before family. Fortunately he had been blessed with a very resourceful wife. And the children are a credit to the family name.

After thirty-five years Frank was finally ready to retire. He dreamt of spending long evenings and weekends getting reacquainted with his loving wife.

On the afternoon of his scheduled retirement party he was making some last-minute changes to the speech he was to give that evening. It was a speech that told a number of stories and anecdotes spelling out the sacrifices that his family had made to further his career. He ended his presentation by asking his wife for her forgiveness and pledging that things would be different in the future now that he was slowing down. Unfortunately, Frank's speech was never given.

The party was scheduled for 7 p.m. At 5, his secretary found Frank slumped over his desk—dead from a heart attack. He and his wife never got to spend those quiet evenings together. If Frank had it all to do over, I wonder if he would have made changes.

How about you? You may be a salesman, an owner of a small business, a retail manager, a tradesman, or a professional. You may hold more than one job or you may be going back to complete your education while holding down a full-time day job. You and your wife may both be caught in the rat race. I know couples who are both so weary and burnt out that they have little to give each other, much less their children, at night or even on the weekends.

I was speaking at a Christian school recently during a parent's day celebration. While waiting my turn at the podium, I overheard a first-grade girl ask a classmate's mother if she would be the girl's mother for the day. The first-grader said *her* mother could not be there because she had to work. I had a hard time getting through my presentation that day. I would have liked to gather that little girl in my arms and be her daddy—at least for that special day.

I do not know all the circumstances that prevented the little girl's parents from attending that important morning. But as I look around at how we live our lives today I wonder if we really need all those "things." Do we need a TV and a VCR in every bedroom or a Walkman for every family member? What has happened to family talks, quiet times together, board games, and picnics with the grandparents? How much money does it take to be successful at the job of being a father?

When *is* enough enough? Do we really need that extra sale, that new customer? Can't we get it done by phone rather than taking another out-of-town business trip? Do we really have to bring work home at night or take that extra job on the weekend?

Make the commitment now to take time for you and your wife to think about this very important issue. When do we stop accumulating and turn our attention to investing in our children and grandchildren?

Not me but thee. God comes first, then family, and then others. After that, I'm sure there will still be a little time for me. I can live the joy-filled life when I have my priorities in order, a fuller understanding of what success is to me, and a plan to redirect my energy and talents after I have determined when enough is enough. Let's pray that we are able to allow God into our lives in such a manner that we can become the men of *velvet and steel* that he intends us to be.

Discussion Questions

1. Are you willing to review your checkbook and calendar with your wife?

2. Do you need to make changes in how you invest your money and time? They are gifts from God, you know.

3. Who and what comes first in your life? Are you willing to die for your family—daily?

4. Are there habits, commitments, or other areas of your life that you need to examine and perhaps change?

5. What value do you place on your children's development? What are their chances of becoming all that God wants them to be?

6. Are you aware that God holds fathers responsible for the spiritual and emotional growth of their families? How do you think you're doing? Will your wife agree with you?

7. Pick out the "Dad" on the next page that you believe your children will identify as you. Then if you have the courage, show it to your children and your wife.

8. Complete the exercise on page 28. Work through your definition of success. Don't be afraid to be truthful. We all have work to do and improvements to make. It is a continuing pilgrimage.

Exercise

Are you willing to pay the price?

How important are the following? (Rank from 1 to 10)

_____ career

_____ sports

_____ time alone

_____ social activities

_____ hobbies

_____ friends

_____ church activities

_____ community

Are you paying too high a price for any of the above?

What is your definition of success?

How important are the following? (Rank from 1 to 10)

_____ career advancement

_____ wealth

_____ community position

_____ social recognition

_____ material possessions

_____ family development

_____ spiritual growth

Using the above rankings, spell out your own definition of success:

Does this definition indicate that you are headed in the right direction?

4

Relationships: Me and Thee

As a business man responsible for bottom line performance, I was not able to handle every customer, make every sale, handle each problem, or make every decision. My job was to make the right things happen through other people. Relationships, working with and through others, were critical to my success. If I could not make my business relationships work well, I would fail as a manager.

Not only was I responsible for those relationships that I could deal with face to face, but I also spent much time and effort negotiating and ironing out differences between staff members. I often used a phrase I picked up years ago to describe the issue: "There are no real problems, just people."

People who cannot get along with one another are major obstacles to business progress. Our organization spent many hours and large amounts of resources on training people to properly handle relationships, to develop interpersonal skills, and to acquire the ability to listen and hear one another. Staff members who could work well with others succeeded. Those who couldn't failed.

Family, with its extended members, is much like a business. Its success or failure will depend upon how the interpersonal relationships work. One of the most important skills you and I can pass on to our children is the ability to get along with others!

Healthy relationships are key to our performance as father/grandfather, role model, and example to our children. If my own family ties are not sound, it is difficult to pass on relational principles to my children. They need to see me working at and maintaining solid relationships with other family members. If those relationships are damaged or broken, they will be looking to see how I am going to mend them. Again, our children do not expect us to be perfect.

29

What we need to pass on is our desire to heal, to understand, and to forgive and our willingness to compromise when necessary.

There are three general areas of relationships for us to examine and work through:

1. my family and me

2. my wife and me

3. my God and me

My Family and Me

While in Chicago, I joined a small group of men that met every Saturday morning. One of the most faithful participants was named Doug. Doug was in his middle forties, was married, and had three daughters. He was a mechanical engineer with a masters degree from Notre Dame. He held an executive engineering position with the local office of a national company. Doug seemed successful, enjoyed a six-figure income, had a close family who loved one another, and had a solid relationship with the Lord. What more could he have desired?

As I became acquainted with the members of my group, I noticed that once a month Doug would be absent. At first I paid little attention, but over time it became apparent that on the Saturday following his absence he appeared to be depressed. I wondered why he experienced such mood swings. He would be up for a week or two and then be quiet and withdrawn the next time I saw him.

I eventually found out Doug struggled with a broken relationship with his father. Doug's father, a retired coal miner, lived alone in western Pennsylvania in the small town where Doug was raised. The father, who had not finished grade school, was bitter and angry about all the years he had labored in the coal mines. He felt that he had been robbed of his youth and the opportunity to succeed by an early marriage and the children who soon followed. He saw in Doug everything he had wanted for himself but had been unable to attain. But instead of feeling proud of his son's accomplishments he was jealous. This rejection had begun when Doug was still in high school. Doug received no help from his family as he worked his way through undergraduate school and on to obtain his master's degree with honors. He did all this on his own.

Doug loved his dad and needed his acceptance. He longed to hear his father say that he loved him and was proud of him. In a situation such as this, most of us would try for a breakthrough, but if we weren't successful, we would probably write off the relationship. For us and for our families, Dad would probably become a non-event, someone to whom we sent cards at Christmas and birthdays, but little else.

Not Doug. Month after month, year after year, he would drive or fly the 1,600-mile round trip over a weekend to visit his father, who lived alone. Doug would faithfully see to his needs, trying once again to earn his father's love, acceptance, and respect. Visit after visit he would return depressed after being rejected and belittled by an angry old man who was living out his last years in bitterness.

Doug then accepted a transfer to manage one of his corporation's plants located in South Carolina. I lost track of him for almost two years, until one Sunday he and his family reappeared at church. They had been transferred back to Chicago and were in the process of moving.

We got together after the service and chatted for a few minutes about family and business. It was good to see him again. Finally I asked the big question. How was his dad?

Doug's face lit up as he smiled and shared that his father had died six months earlier. I was a bit taken aback by his comment, but as he continued, his meaning became clear. Due to the onset of Alzheimer's disease, his father's memory had begun to fade soon after Doug moved to South Carolina. All the bitter memories of the past, the resentment and jealousy, had melted into oblivion. And then, for the last nine months of his life, Doug and his dad enjoyed the loving father-son relationship that Doug had always longed for. Those few happy months erased the scars of half a lifetime. Doug felt a release, the lifting of a heavy burden. He was a whole man, okay with the present, at peace with the past.

We all need the acceptance and love of significant people in our lives. For men, the relationship with our own fathers is a critical one. Doug had the respect and acceptance of his immediate family, his business associates, and his church community, but it wasn't enough. He desperately needed his own earthly father to take him in his arms and tell him that he was loved and that Dad was proud of his son.

You and I may tell others that we're tough, stand-alone men, but it just isn't so.

One of the first exercises during the Effective Father Seminars is to have dads and grandfathers think about their relationship with their own fathers. We give them a few minutes for review and then ask for volunteers to share either their memories or current relationship with their father.

Over the years, the groups seem to split approximately into thirds. One third will testify to a supporting and loving father—a man who was there, who was a listener and a powerful role model. This group looks up to their fathers for help even now as they are dealing with their own children. He is a partner, a helper, the kind of grandfather his children need.

Another third usually began the description of their father with a phrase that goes something like "Dad worked hard." He really was "a good man and a good provider." He was, what I call, an absent-but-accounted-for dad. He was a father

"Dad worked hard."

who often traveled on business and spent large blocks of time away from home. Or he was at home but unavailable, often tied to other interests such as sports, TV, or hobbies. Dad was not a positive developmental force in his son's life. Even today his sons do not see him as a resource or helper in their children's development. This father was, and remains, a non-event, a fact that their sons resent.

The men in the last group often have a look of anger on their faces when they share that dad deserted his family. These dads often drank, couldn't hold a job, were unfaithful, left their family through divorce or abandonment, or, worst of all, abused them.

Once one father is courageous enough to share, others begin to open up with similar stories—stories of hurt, anger, and unforgiveness. Often these memories and feelings have lain dormant for years. They need to be exposed and dealt with for the healing process to begin.

When scheduling a seminar in a church, I alert the pastor to the fact that we will be discussing broken relationships and that we will need his support. Healing these men often requires extended counseling. We ask the pastor to provide this counseling or to be ready to refer men seeking help to the proper resources.

If abuse is part of your family history and you have not as yet dealt with it, make the commitment to do so. Your children deserve a dad who is healed and whole.

What about dads who realize, often after the children have left home, that they have been less than a man of velvet and steel?

A man in his middle fifties attended a seminar a few years ago. After the initial session he remained and asked for ten minutes of my time. After an hour and a half we broke up and made a date to work again after the session the following week.

He began to tell his story with tears in his eyes. He and his wife have four daughters, all grown, with families of their own. Three of his daughters now live some distance away. Although the daughters have ongoing communication with their mother, Dad is not included. A wall has been built up over the years. Each daughter, in her own way, wants little or nothing to do with her father.

Dad is now paying the price for years of priorities that did not include his girls. He assured me that there was no abuse, just neglect, as he pleaded for help on how to get his daughters and grandchildren back. We prayed together and then discussed first steps on what could be a very long road. It may take years and even then he may never be totally successful. He agreed that the first step toward healing was to say how sorry he is and that he knows he was wrong. It's not the time to ask for anything—let alone forgiveness. For now it's enough to say "I'm sorry."

For now it's enough to say "I'm sorry."

Since his daughters won't even speak with him, we began with a short, simple letter in which he acknowledged his shortcomings and past errors and confessed his sorrow. Over the following weeks he and I constructed a series of follow-up letters individualized for each daughter—the issues were a bit different in each case. During the six-week class a small breakthrough took place with one of his daughters. A start was made with the simple words, "I'm sorry." I often wonder why it takes us so long to say those two little words.

Most conflicts can be resolved if dealt with on a timely basis. Family counselors agree that families should never allow the sun to set on disagreements. The following story illustrates the truth of this.

During the summer of 1996 Rita and I put together a trip for our family to the Grand Tetons and Yellowstone National Park. Eighteen of us met in Denver for two days and then filled the rear section of a United Airlines 737 for a flight into Jackson, Wyoming.

Our children and their spouses gathered with our eight grandchildren for a week of fun and togetherness. Making family memories, maintaining and strengthening bonds among our children's families, are high priorities for Rita and myself. We try to bring the whole crew together at least twice a year. It takes planning and sacrifice, but we think the results, especially for the grandchildren, are worth the price.

But there are challenges. Four adult siblings, very different from one another, mixed with spouses who come from various backgrounds add up to an interesting opportunity for either pleasant experiences or disasters. It is understood that there can never be complete agreement on anything. Where and when our gatherings are to be held and what we will do when we get there must be built around give-and-take attitudes. Even picking a starting time in the morning can be a challenge. Some are late risers while others are early birds.

We try to include everyone's wishes and preferences, but that is not always possible. An attitude of mutual acceptance with all our individual baggage is key to our success. No one will be completely happy all the time, but so what! We're together and that's really what counts. The younger generation is building ties that we hope will last a lifetime. We are trying to be an example of how family can succeed and I believe the results are worth the effort.

> **As family, we are expected to accept each other, just as we are.**

That is not to say that we never have conflicts. We do! This last trip was no exception. If you can remember the great blackout in the western states on the third of July, 1996, you can appreciate the setting: eighteen people, no electricity, no shops or restaurants open, no TV, and no lights.

We decided to jump into our two vans and take off for Yellowstone (sixty-five miles one way) to view wildlife at dusk. We left at 5 p.m. and drove, and drove and drove. After a stop or two we reached the park at 7:30 p.m. If we were to see bison, elk, and moose it would mean another hour's drive into the park. The picnic dinner we had planned had come apart somewhere along the way. The kids had gotten hungry and we allowed them to eat as we drove along. The prospect of another hour in the vans with all those kids, not to mention the return trip home, was just too much. It was time to head back. Hours in the vans, no real dinner, no animals, just a lot of togetherness!

By the time we returned to our villa, tempers had flared, feelings were hurt, the trip was a disaster, and the family, at midnight, had been pushed past their limit. I allowed the sun to set!

At Bible study next morning we discussed the prior evening's fiasco but group therapy was not enough. Individuals paired off for private talks and by 9 a.m. we were almost back to normal. A poorly planned and executed evening—by yours truly—would now be a memory we could laugh about in coming years. No permanent damage had been done. Repair work had been done quickly.

Individuals, even within the same family, are just that—individual and unique. Each of us has a different approach to child rearing, career planning, and lifestyle. As family, we are expected to accept each other just as we are.

If there is damage to repair, begin the healing process by saying, "I'm sorry. Let's talk." Invite Jesus Christ into your conversation and, if needed, seek professional help—I suggest you begin with your pastor. And keep in mind that men of velvet and steel are called to take the first step.

My Wife and Me

Society paints the picture of a successful man as self-sufficient, a self-starter, the Clint Eastwood type—a solitary figure on horseback leaving a town he has just cleaned up with at least one woman begging him to stay.

You and I are not Clint Eastwood. We probably don't even ride a horse. But we can identify with much of Clint's general description. The vast majority of us are individuals with few, if any, close male friends. We view other men, including our own fathers, as competitors who are not completely trustworthy. We carry our problems within, which too often leads to stress-related health problems. Whom should we talk to? Open up to? Share our lives with? The logical answer is our wives—for whom we've confessed our undying love and to whom we've committed our lives. They are our lovers, the mothers of our children, the intimate partners who share our dreams.

But your wife will more than likely tell you that you don't share. In fact she may often ask the question, "Why won't you talk to me? Why aren't you interested in my hopes and dreams? We just don't seem to understand each other." Much of what our wives complain about is true. Why *are* we the way we are? The answer is that we men *do not know how* to open up and share ourselves. We don't even know how to listen well. We have had few, if any, role models to emulate. Our own fathers probably did not open up to us or even to our mothers, so we have had no one from whom to learn.

Unless you and your wife are completely satisfied with your marriage, I strongly suggest that you take advantage of some of the many resources available to help couples communicate. One that you might find helpful is *The Covenant Experience: 11 Steps to a Better Marriage* by Bob and Irene Tomonto and Myrna Gallagher (Resource Publications, Inc., 1995). Check with your pastor or other church leaders for other suggestions.

The vast majority of our seminar attendees states that they and their wives often have difficulty coming to agreement about basic family life issues. Children develop a deeper sense of confidence in themselves when their mother and father operate as team in love with one another and their children and who display that love openly.

Father Theodore Hesburgh, retired president of the University of Notre Dame, has stated that "the most important gift a father can give his children is to love their mother."

God, speaking to us through Paul in Ephesians tells us, "Husbands should love their wives, just as Christ loved the Church and sacrificed himself for her…" (Ep 5:25).

Earlier in this book we shared a story about an apartment fire. The husband sacrificed his life so that his wife, the mother of his children, might live. This sacrificial theme is repeated over and over again in Scripture. You and I are commissioned to lay ourselves down, in love, for those whom God has entrusted to our care—our wives and children.

In order to better illustrate how a husband should love his wife, I've taken liberties with 1 Corinthians 13 as found in the Living Bible (Tyndale House, 1971):

> The love of a husband for his wife is very patient and kind, never jealous or envious, never boastful or proud, never haughty or rude. His love is not selfish and does not demand its own way. It is not irritable or touchy. It does not hold grudges and will hardly even notice when his wife does it wrong. Husband, if you love your wife, you will be loyal at all costs, you will always believe in her, always expect the best of her, and always stand your ground in defending her.

In the following table I outline Paul's "do and do nots" of loving one's spouse.

DO:	DO NOT:
be patient	be demanding
be kind	be rude
be lovingly unselfish	be superior
be loyal	be jealous
believe in her	hold a grudge
expect the best	be haughty
be forgiving	be self-centered
defend her	be out of sorts

As I went over this list with my wife, Rita, she was lovingly loyal and most kind as she gave me the passing grade of C+.

There were numerous occasions when I was guilty of the "do nots." Central to my failures was the need to have my own way in the major events of our life together.

Over the years I accepted five transfers, all without Rita's informed input. Once I even revealed a move from St. Louis to Chicago by phone to her hospital room as she was recovering from major surgery. It took nerve, but I was equal to the task. You see, I wanted that promotion badly. The move involved leaving our four grown children and two grandchildren. The real issue, however, was that I did not take the time to fully explain the pros and cons and allow Rita to think and pray about the decision. Why didn't I seek my partner's counsel? She is a bright, intelligent woman with many skills and insights, different but complementary to my own. It was because I wanted to make the move. I was set in my decision and was not willing to discuss, reflect, or compromise.

The model relationship for husbands and wives is one of full partnership in which both partners respect each other, are open to arriving at joint decisions and operate in a give-and-take atmosphere. The resulting decisions, are wholeheartedly owned by both partners, each deferring to the other in areas of their spouse's expertise.

I am a planner—more of a long-term decision maker. As a banker, many of my skills are in the area of finance. I am outgoing, a risk taker, a free spender, a social person. Rita is complementary in that she is creative, somewhat shy, conservative, and a saver. Before she leaps, she wants to have at least "most" of the answers. I ofttimes become frustrated by her simple, searching questions concerning purchases or planned vacations. Her questions often make me reexamine my direction. She invariably makes me rethink and dig a bit deeper before we commit. Rita steadies my quick hand. Together we add up to much more than we are individually. And then with God as the head of our partnership, we are ready to provide the sound foundation that our children and grandchildren need. Together we *three* are more than a match for the evil, self-centered values of today's society. Our children are able to believe in a loving God because they have experienced his unconditional love in their parents' love for each other and for them.

Therefore, you can see that we are called to love our wives, respect them, honor and defend them. But are we ready to open up the lines of communication and deeply share with them?

Men often bring up the fact that coming to an agreement with their wives on anything is almost impossible. Different family backgrounds and experiences make such agreements a real challenge for today's couple. I would

4. Relationships: Me and Thee

suggest that these differences might be more readily resolved if husbands and wives will *talk, listen, share, and hear* on a regular basis.

I was raised in St. Louis, Missouri, in a mixed neighborhood of Irish Catholic and Jewish families. (We were the exception.) Our family had no TV, one radio, and no air conditioning. During long summer evenings, neighborhood children would play until after dark while parents sat on their porches and talked. The parents had no agenda, no discussion list, no written plan—they just talked. They talked about us kids, their jobs, their extended families, news events and sports. But most of all they shared their lives with one another. When we *talk and listen often*, it soon becomes natural to begin to *share and hear*. Sharing and hearing is the next level of verbal intimacy.

> **If husbands and wives don't decide to make time for one another, it won't happen.**

Our own children often marvel at Rita and me. I have a habit of beginning a sentence and then losing my train of thought half-way through. Rita will pick it up right where I left off and finish it for me. She and I can hear music, look at a photo, smell a fragrance, or hear a sound and recall the same event which might have taken place years ago. We are tuned to the same frequency. We almost know what the other is thinking before opening our mouths. This comes naturally because we have talked and listened for forty years. However, we have only recently begun to *share and hear*.

Talking, listening, sharing, and hearing won't happen without our decision to make it happen.

Our four children are all married with children of their own. Two families have chosen to live on a single income. The other two families have working mothers—one part-time, one full-time. All are busy with the challenges of daily life. School, church, sports, and home activities are all good and necessary, but they all take time. If husbands and wives don't *decide* to make time for one another, it won't happen.

Laura, our firstborn, and her husband, Keven, have set aside one evening a week as "date night." That evening alone with one another is a high priority in their weekly schedule. Sometimes they put special issues for discussion on the evening's agenda, but there is always time to just talk.

Talking and listening will happen only if we *make* it happen. Sharing and hearing require a deeper level of trust, understanding, and empathy. An hour or two over dinner isn't really enough time, nor is it the proper setting for heart-sharing. Regular overnights, or even better, weekends alone, can help to foster and encourage deeper levels of communication.

Many couples never reach those levels because they have no one to care for the children while they are away. Your church community may provide the answer. I am sure there are couples, just like you, who need to get away by themselves from time to time. Perhaps you could trade weekends with a couple you know and respect, watching their children one weekend and having them care for yours the next.

Children respond favorably to parents who talk, listen, share, and hear.

Grandparents can help too. Rita and I recently spent a week with our eight-year-old grandson, Chris, while his parents went skiing together.

Solid communication between couples is vital to their role as parents and crucial to their children's development. Children respond favorably to a husband-wife relationship that talks, listens, shares, and hears.

Earlier we discussed setting priorities in order to better understand where our family is headed. How we are to invest our God-given talents, time, and resources is a question we all need to answer. It is a question that needs to be answered jointly, by both husband and wife. They need to talk, listen, and pray together in order to arrive at *God's* direction for their family.

Most of us allow career decisions to be made for us. I entered the financial field almost by mistake. I answered a newspaper ad calling for an investigator. I pictured myself in an exciting private eye career armed with camera and listening device. I had no idea of where that first job—which was in fact collecting delinquent car payments for a local bank—would take me. But indeed the industry we choose to enter can determine all kinds of life issues, not only for the present but far into the future. Overtime, travel requirements, weekend meetings, shift work, transfers, etc., are but a few of the job attributes that can determine how we live.

As mentioned earlier, our son, Kevin, is a civil engineer who builds hospitals. His job assignments can last anywhere from one to three years. With each new assignment, he is required to move. Each move means a new town, a new community, a new church, and a new school for their son, Christopher. Chris is eight years old. The frequent moves have not as yet been a problem for him. However, I'm sure that as he approaches his teen years and high school, the moves will become more difficult. Kevin and Belinda, after discussing this at length, have made the decision that Kevin's career should permit them to settle in a permanent hometown before Chris begins his teenage years. They have five or six years to make that happen.

Communication is the key to a parenting partnership that works.

permit them to settle in a permanent hometown before Chris begins his teenage years. They have five or six years to make that happen.

Planning ahead can certainly help to divert problems before they occur. A corporate pilot who attended a seminar several years ago was having major problems with a teenage son. His frequent overnight travel was, in his estimation, a contributing factor to his son's problems. He was seldom there to handle disciplinary issues as they arose.

His career was a major obstacle to the overall well being of his family. Although he and I spent several hours developing stop-gap plans, his career remained a real issue. More than once he confessed that he wished he had never embarked upon a career as a pilot. There were other ways he could have used his skills in the aviation industry, ways which would have allowed him more time at home.

Career plans, children's education, and where the family will live are a few of the major decisions a husband and wife should jointly decide early in their marriage. Don't let life's events take control and decide these important issues for you. You and your wife make those decisions pro-actively, not re-actively.

God's order for couples is a loving— talk, listen, share, and hear—partnership. With Jesus Christ as the center of their lives, parents prayerfully decide down which path they want to lead their children.

Your wife is your best friend, your confessor, your lover, a partner with whom to share your life. Don't lock her out!

By now you understand that communication is a vitally important part of any successful marriage. It is the key to a parenting partnership that works.

What we have been discussing is a union in which the marriage is still intact—in which the husband and wife are working together as a team while living together as man and wife. Over the years, however, the number of single dads who attend the seminar has increased dramatically. Fathers, most of whom are not the custodial parent, come seeking help on how to be a better, more effective father. Often they are also looking for an avenue to reclaim their wife and make a new start.

Although the intent of this book is not one of marriage counseling, single fathers may, however, pick up a few hints along the way.

As we shared before, the first step toward forgiveness and healing in any relationship is to say, "I'm sorry. Sorry for all the times I didn't measure up. Sorry for all the times I let the family down." That first step is to say those words unconditionally and without expecting a response.

> ## "I'm sorry for all the times I didn't measure up."

Saying "I'm sorry" won't help much, though, unless it is meant sincerely. There are two sides, two points of view, to every unsuccessful marriage. Deeply rooted problems and misunderstandings that caused the marriage to fail will not be resolved overnight. Months, even years, of behavioral and attitudinal change are often necessary before a level of trust can be rebuilt.

In the meantime, the welfare of your children remains the highest priority for you as their father. By beginning with the words "I'm sorry," a path can be cleared for you and your former spouse to begin to dialogue for the good of the children.

Regular open talking and listening between you and your children's mother is vitally important to the sound development of your sons and daughters. Peaceful talks, talks in which you share issues and problems and develop joint plans of action, will provide the consistency that will encourage your children to thrive.

Even if you found it difficult to operate as a team while married, your kids deserve the sacrificial commitment from both of their parents to work together. Being able to rely and hold onto a father-mother team, even one that is physically separated, is a priceless gift for any child. You may be thinking this is impossible. You did not get along as a married couple, how can it be expected that you succeed as a team now. You are right; it will be difficult. But it can be possible through your unselfish desire to make it work for the sake of your children. There is also a verse in Scripture that you might like to hold on to; Luke 1:37 tell us that "nothing is impossible with God."

In his book, *Single Parents* (Tyndale House, 1992), Bob Barnes discusses children's bedtime as a non-threatening issue for a couple who is separated. If the children are with their father on weekends, coming to an agreement with their mother about bedtime can lead to more important joint decisions later. Start small and build toward future meaningful discussions.

Here are a few pointers gleaned from my work with single fathers, along with a few suggestions from Dr. Barnes' book:

1. No spying. Refrain from asking your children searching questions about their mother.

2. Don't put the kids in the middle and ask them to choose sides. What your former spouse does now is her own business, even if you believe it is affecting the children. Your good example will do more to improve their developmental atmosphere than taking pot-shots at your ex's lifestyle.

3. No bad mouthing. No negative comments. No passing judgment. If you must talk about your past marriage, share the good times and build up your ex-wife. Remember, your children are carrying around a load of guilt. They may even believe they are responsible for the breakup of your marriage. Be sure they know nothing could be farther from the truth. The proof is in the fact that you and their mother, even with your deep differences, are working together because of your mutual love for them. They are the most precious gift that came from your marriage union.

Single parenting is, without a doubt, difficult. But your children are crying for their mother and father to love them and work as a team, even when they are no longer together as a couple.

God and Me

Recently I met with a close friend. He is a successful business man, a father, and an active church member. As we talked he confided that his life, while full and active, was not the fulfilled, peaceful life he longed for. He truly wanted to experience what Scripture refers to as "that peace that passes understanding" (Ph 4:7).

I asked if he would like to hear about my own search for that "full and abundant life" (Jn 10:10) and he was quite pleased that I would share my story with him.

I told him I had come to understand that there are three great questions that face each one of us.

1. What is the meaning of this life we live? Have we humans risen from prehistoric muck to live out our seventy-five or so years and then pass into oblivion?

2. Is there really a God who created us and everything else in this so-called universe? Is he the loving, almighty God that church and Scripture would have us believe, or is it all a myth conjured up to satisfy man's desire for that *something more*?

3. Is Jesus Christ who he says he is?

I went on to tell my friend that I had found all other questions and issues of life almost irrelevant in the light of these three. What is life about? Who is God? Who is Jesus Christ? To answer those questions, let me share my pilgrimage, my own search for the answers.

My wife Rita and I originally come from the Midwest. My father, Edward, a research chemist, and my mother, Thelma, a teacher, had a stormy five-year marriage that ended in divorce. Although I was only three, I remember the shouting, the anger, and how frightened I was. You cannot tell me that the breakup of a marriage does not produce scarred children.

Mother and I went to live with my grandparents. While I have a few fond memories of my grandfather, I remember those years as very tough for my mother. She worked as a teacher, received very little support from my dad, and lived in someone else's home.

When I was about six, mother began to date the man who was the principal at the school where she taught, and in June of 1941, she married James Ream. We then moved as a family into a small apartment in St. Louis. Then World War II came, and although my stepfather was thirty-five years old and blind in one eye, he was drafted into the army air force. He ended up in England and served there throughout the remainder of the war.

After the war, in 1945, we were back together again, along with my new half-sister, Harriet, who was born while Dad Ream was away in England. We were ready to begin what we all hoped would be a long and happy life together.

One day in 1947 I noticed Mother taping a gauze bandage over an open sore on her left breast. I was twelve or thirteen at the time, and although I was concerned, the gravity of the situation escaped me. Mom had contracted breast cancer and since she was a member of the Christian Science Church, she did not seek, nor did she accept, medical assistance. The next two years were indeed painful for all of us. Mother's cancer metastasized throughout her body and settled in her bones. She lived out her final year hospitalized in a waist-high body cast, in terrible pain, eased only by regular doses of narcotics every few hours. Dad Ream spent every night with her, sleeping in a chair by her bed in the small hospital room. At fourteen, it was my responsibility to take care of my four-year-old sister, Harriet. It was a tough time for all of us.

Mom died in October of 1949 at the age of forty-three. She was a highly intelligent, gracious, giving lady, who unfortunately had experienced much pain and suffering during her relatively short life.

God is also the God of economics and business.

Although Dad Ream was a fine man, we *never* had a father-son relationship. We were so very different that we found it virtually impossible to communicate. At fifteen I was motherless, hurt, confused. I dropped out of high school. After a six-month stint as a stock-boy at a local department store, I left home and joined the Marine Corps.

God was not part of my life at that time. My mother had trusted in something and it had not worked. Why should I trust in the same thing?

I grew and matured during the next three years as a U.S. Marine. I can highly recommend the Marine Corps to today's youth, for the Marines foster pride, a sense of self-worth, the ability to operate as a team member, and of course, discipline. That experience has helped me throughout the years.

Upon my discharge, I tried college for a couple of years, ran out of money, and went to work for a subsidiary of the Bank of St. Louis. I collected accounts and repossessed automobiles.

In 1956 I met Rita on a blind date. She was a high quality person and came from a loving family. We were married seven months later. As a concession to her and her widowed mother, I joined their church. I became a Roman Catholic. But going to church on Sundays became just a habit. It was what decent people did on Sunday mornings after reading the comics and the sport page. I obeyed church rules and even prayed a bit, but God was always something or somebody not quite real to me. Even if he was real I was sure he could not be interested in someone like me.

Rita and I moved from St. Louis to Houston shortly after our marriage. Our four children were born there. Later we transferred to Atlanta, where I had responsibility for several states. Although we were not rich, we were making solid progress. We had a nice new home that came with a nice new mortgage. My business future looked bright. I became active at our church and began doing lots of *good* things. I helped with the landscaping, worked on installing a new roof, and sat on various committees. I must confess, though, that my motives were more personal than spiritual. Looking back, I would say that I had a "front yard" ministry. I was more interested in being seen and in who could benefit me career-wise than in any spiritual development. I wanted to work in that "front yard" so that others could see what a good person and church member I was.

In her early thirties and with our children in school, Rita soon became restless. Although we had a happy marriage and a good social life, she began to search out the answer to that question, "Is this all there is?"

At first she looked in all the wrong places. She spent two years dabbling in the occult, astrology and reincarnation, reading numerous books on the subjects, and doing some pretty weird things. Although her actions made me uneasy I didn't see any real harm in them if they kept her occupied and happy. Little by little, though, Rita became disillusioned with all that until she finally, by the grace of God, turned her back on it altogether. We settled back once again into our suburban routine of work, church, parties, little league, and PTA.

Jesus seemed to be taking my place as the center of Rita's life.

Then early in 1970 Rita's mother called. She was upset and asked Rita to fly to St. Louis and help bring her two sisters, who were involved in a home prayer group, back to reality. Rita went for about ten days. When she returned, Rita had a glow about her.

Thus began the most trying year in our then fifteen years of marriage. Rita came home to Atlanta and her family a changed woman, for she had encountered Jesus Christ in a very real and personal way. For her it was a life-changing event. She tried to share her experience with me, but I refused to listen. I thought that she was probably just going through another of her "occult" phases. Wasn't church on Sunday enough? What was it with all the praying and Bible reading? She even drove sixty miles, regularly, to attend some sort of prayer meeting.

Not only did I not understand, but I started to become jealous of all the time and attention this *Jesus fellow* was receiving. He seemed to be taking my place as the center of Rita's life, and I did not understand, nor did I like it one little bit.

Finally after a visit to our home by Terry, one of her "Jesus freak" sisters, I had had enough. I told Rita that it was either Jesus or me one of us had to go. She took my ultimatum, thought about it for a day or two, and came back to me with the promise that she would never speak of Jesus again in my presence. She said that she could never go back to the way she was before but that I would never have to see or hear about it again. She also stopped attending the weekly gatherings. All this made me feel a little guilty. I regretted my stern attitude and wondered why there could not be some sort of middle ground. Did it have to be all or nothing at all? As a peace offering, I agreed to attend a weekend retreat for men, being held by some of her Christian friends. I went off to that weekend on a

"I'm sorry.
Let's talk."

Thursday evening late in February 1971, not knowing what to expect and certainly not prepared for what I experienced.

The retreat team was made up of businessmen like myself. During the three days they prepared meals, spent time on their knees, and gave personal talks describing the Gospel of Jesus Christ as the ultimate and only answer for a fulfilled life here on earth. Although I had heard it from the pulpit many times over the years, for the first time it became clear to me that God the Father, his Son, Jesus, and the Holy Spirit love me just like I am and have a unique and exciting plan for my life.

I was deeply impressed by the depth of sharing that weekend. These were *real* men discussing and praying about *real* problems while living successful *real* lives. It wasn't that they were without issues, concerns, hurts, or troubled relationships, for those things were indeed evident in the talks they gave. However, I came to realize that their approach was different, that there was a spiritual peacefulness in how these men handled their day-to-day living. Two Scripture passages that they used over and over again during that weekend became real to me. Both are from the Gospel of St. John. The first is John 10:10, in which Jesus proclaims that he has come to give us life, the *abundant* life. The second is John 14:27: "Peace I bequeath to you, my own peace I give you, a peace which the world cannot give, this is my gift to you. Do not let not your hearts be troubled or afraid."

As I drove home on Sunday evening after the closing ceremony of the retreat, I prayerfully made the commitment to God and myself that Rita and I would invite Jesus Christ to take his rightful place at the center of our marriage and our family. That evening at home, after the kids were asleep, we prayed for the first time as a couple. Kneeling down beside our bed we made that commitment a reality.

The church and Christian community took on new meaning for me. I knew I could not make it by myself. Sure I was developing a prayer life, reading, studying, and praying the Scriptures, but I also needed to be with people who were open and willing to share the ups and downs of *their* Christian walk. Our determination to grow in our faith ultimately resulted in our involvement with retreat work. Thus, I became an active worker in the very process that God used to reach me.

As our family life moved in a new direction, I began to see that the greatest gift I could give my children was to introduce them to the person of Jesus Christ, both by word and example. For them to develop a living faith of their own, they needed an earthly father who was walking hand in hand with their heavenly Father.

In 1973 my company became part of Citicorp, the largest and most profitable bank based in the United States. I was transferred back to St. Louis, which was the site of our national mortgage bank. With increased responsibilities, I was now leading the mortgage branch business for the eastern half of the United States. I have always been proud to work for Citicorp, for they maintained a working and business environment based on the highest set of ethical values and ideals. However, as a Christian I was called to push it just a bit further. Those I worked with,

The need today for effective, godly fathers is greater than ever before.

including my boss, always knew for what and whom I stood. How we treated and valued the customer, and each other, was special. As a Christian, a follower of Jesus Christ, I am called to be different, even in the business world. Since Jesus is a *gentle man* with a peace-filled Gospel message, I never forced my faith on others. But the manner in which our business was managed led to numerous opportunities to counsel with employees and customers alike. Most of these encounters revolved around relationship issues involving family.

Although my superiors knew of my beliefs, I never ran into any resistance from them. I have to believe that God blessed our efforts with sound financial results that made it difficult for them to find fault with our operations. Once, while in New York for a business conference, I was seated at dinner next to one of our senior human resource officers. As we introduced ourselves, he remarked from across the table, "Oh you're that Christian fellow who runs our bank in Chicago, the one with the good numbers!" Yes, we march to a different drummer, but our God is also the God of economics and business. The basic truths of Christianity work just as well in his world of commerce. Be not afraid to stand up and speak out for what you believe. My experience reinforces the reality that God will smile and bless your efforts.

Now that I am retired from the bank, I am delighted to have the time to devote full attention to Christian ministry for fathers. Our children *need* heroes they can look up to and emulate. The need *today* for *effective, godly fathers* is greater than ever before. There just aren't many heroes left out there.

I began this sharing by laying out three questions for your consideration. *What is this life on earth all about?* It is not about financial wealth or possessions. It is about relationships. It's about a God-centered relationship that makes all other relationships work. It is about a loving God who existed before the "Big Bang" and who longs to be invited into the innermost reaches of our heart. It is about the "Good Shepherd," Jesus Christ, who truthfully proclaimed that he is indeed the Way, the Truth, and the Life. My prayer for each of you is that you might seek out that truth and answer those three questions for yourself.

In Matthew 16:15, Jesus asks Peter, "Who do you say I am?" My friends, who do you say Jesus Christ is? Is he the Lord of your life? Is he your role model? You and I are called to be different—a beacon in this dark world—a light that our children might find their way.

Sound relationships are a key element as we become men of *velvet and steel*. Solid ties with our past, our extended family, our wife, and our God are vital in knowing who we are and where we are going. We will never actually arrive, for we are on a continuing journey, a never-ending struggle to become the men our wives and children need us to be—the man God expects us to be.

Discussion Questions: My Family and Me

1. How would you describe your own relationship with your father? Does it need repair work? If so, how and when will you begin?

2. Grandfathers, how would your sons and daughters answer question one? Do you also have repair work to do?

3. Is there someone in your past that needs your forgiveness? Do you need help in getting started?

Discussion Questions: My Wife and Me

1. Take a few moments to grade yourself on the "dos" and "do nots." Do you need to work on any?

2. Are there incidents and occasions that require an "I'm sorry. Please forgive me"?

3. How does your family make decisions? Are they made by joint agreement?

4. What are your wife's areas of expertise? What are yours? Do you defer to each other's strengths?

5. Do you and your wife make time to talk and listen? Have you moved on to sharing and hearing?

6. Do you know what your wife's dreams are? Would you change your plans to accommodate them?

Single Fathers:

1. Can you put aside you own anger and hurt feelings for the good of your children?

2. Will you take steps toward better communication and joint planning with your ex-wife? Your children deserve it.

Discussion Questions: God and Me

1. Where are you in your relationship with God? Would you call it intimate? close? distant? or non-existent?

2. What would you like it to be?

3. Do you believe that the Father, Son, and Holy Spirit are key elements to successful fathering?

4. Do your children see you pray? Do you pray with them?

5. Who do *you* say Jesus Christ is to your family and friends?

5

It's 10 P.M.
Do You Know Where
Your Children Are?

Keep sober and alert, because *your enemy*, the devil, is on prowl like
a roaring lion, looking for *someone to devour*. Stand up to him,
strong in *faith* and [in the] *knowledge*" (1 P 5:8, emphasis mine).

God's words through Peter are as appropriate for us today as they were
for the Christians of the first century. The evil in today's world is
indeed prowling around looking for someone to devour and, unfortunately, it is zeroing in on our children. We fathers must stand strong and firm
in our faith if we are to succeed in leading our children to safety.

Years ago during active duty with the Marine Corps, I would often pass the
parachute loft. There the parachute riggers packed chutes for pilots and crew.
Although they were highly trained and reliable, flight crew members would often
inspect and sometimes request a repack if they were not completely satisfied with
the look or feel of their chute. Their very lives depended on how well the job was
done. Those airmen chose to "know" rather than to "assume."

Later, as a business manager, I came to understand the danger of that word
"assume." "I just assumed..." was all too often the initial phrase of a failure report.

The reporting subordinate, almost without exception, had not checked,
looked into, verified, established, substantiated, authenticated, tested, or
confirmed a critical operation. And now *we* were going to pay the price. They
had neither taken the time nor made the effort to "know."

Since the bank was my responsibility, I *had* to "know." It was not my goal to know every detail about every department, but I had to "know" enough. I needed to *know enough* to be reasonably certain that the subordinate and I were speaking the same language, using the same vocabulary, and that what I was hearing and seeing was the truth, even if that truth hurt.

In order to be able to sleep at night, I took a business principle of the '80s to heart—"managing by wandering around." I copied the tried-and-true example of top-notch successful business leaders and developed a plan to regularly visit various departments, ask questions, look around, and most importantly, to listen. My job as a leader was "to know."

Gordon MacDonald, in his classic book *The Effective Father* (Tyndale House Publishers, 1977), points out that the Bible tells the stories of two fathers, Eli and Mordecai, in which *knowing, or the lack thereof*, had far-reaching consequences on their families and the people of Israel.

Eli, Israel's chief priest, was a Levite. Since their escape from Egypt, his family had been blessed by God. They had been promised priesthood through future generations. But Eli was not the model of priestly behavior, nor was he the "knowing" father that God had called him to be. Let me share the story's highlights.

The Story of Eli

The Sons of Eli (1 Samuel 2)

Now the sons of Eli were scoundrels; they cared nothing for Yahweh nor for what was due to the priests from the people (1 S 2:12-13).

The young men's sin was very great in Yahweh's eyes, because they treated with contempt the offering made to Yahweh (1 S 2:17).

Although very old, Eli heard about everything that his sons were doing to all Israel, and said, "Why are you behaving as all the people say you are? Know my sons what I hear reported by the people of Yahweh is not good" (1 S 2:22-24)

Key thoughts for us in these passages are:

1. Eli's sons had offended God.

2. Eli had to be told by others of his sons' rebellious behavior.

3. Their rebellion against God and his people had been going on for some time.

It seems that Eli had missed the mark as both priest and father.

Future Punishment Announced to Eli

…Yahweh says, "Did I not reveal myself to your father's house when they were in Egypt as slaves in Pharaoh's household? Did I not single him out of all the tribes of Israel to be my priest…?" (1 S 2:27-28)

Whereas—this is what Yahweh, God of Israel, declares—I had promised that your father and your father's family would walk in my presence for ever, now, however—this is what Yahweh declares—nothing of the sort! Those who honour me I will honour in my turn, and those who despise me will be an object of contempt. Be sure, the days are coming when I shall cut off your strength and the strength of your father's family, so that no one in your family will live to old age (1 S 2:30-31).

"What happens to your two sons Hophni and Phinehas will be a sign for you: on the same day both will die" (1 S 2:34).

Yahweh expected Eli to "know" his sons and to take appropriate action for their rebellious behavior. Hophni and Phinehas needed proper training from their father early in life. While they were growing up they should have had warnings and discipline from him when necessary. Eli failed to follow Yahweh's plan and thus he, his sons, and their future families lost God's blessing. His failure as a father to "know" his sons cost them their lives. Eli and his family paid a great price for their rebellion. Unfortunately, stories much like Eli's are being played out today. Too many fathers are not making the effort to "know" their children.

The Story of Esther and Mordecai

The story of Esther and her stepfather, Mordecai, shows us a very different kind of father-child relationship. It tells of the deliverance of the nation of Israel by the faithful actions of a woman under the direction of her *knowing* stepfather.

The entire book of Esther is well worth taking the time to study. You might review this Old Testament book with your teenage daughters, for it illustrates what is possible when a daughter-father team work together in God's name.

Let's review the highlights from a few selected verses:

Esther Becomes Queen (Esther 2)

...bringing up a certain Hadassah, otherwise called Esther, his
uncle's daughter, who had lost both father and mother; the girl had a
good figure and a beautiful face, and on the death of her parents,
Mordecai had adopted her as his daughter (Est 2:7).

...Esther too, was taken to the king's palace and entrusted to Hegai,
the custodian of the women (Est 2:8).

Esther had not divulged her race or parentage, since Mordecai had
forbidden her to do so. Mordecai walked up and down in front of the
courtyard of the harem every day, to learn how Esther was and how
she was being treated (Est 2:10-11).

...and the king liked Esther better than any of the other women;
none of the other girls found so much favour and approval with him.
So he set the royal diadem on her head and proclaimed her queen...
(Est 2:17).

When Esther, like the other girls, had been transferred to the second
harem, she did not divulge her parentage or race, *in obedience* to the
orders of Mordecai, whose instructions she *continued to follow* as
when she was had been under his care (Est 2:19-20, emphasis mine).

Mordecai adopted his orphaned cousin, Esther, as his own daughter,
probably when she was a child. He performed well as her stepfather. She grew
to be an obedient, well-mannered young lady. Her beauty and demeanor
attracted the king's favor and he chose her as his queen. Although Esther
became royalty, she continued to respect, obey, and follow her stepfather's
directives.

Haman, jealous of Mordecai's rise to power, plots the annihilation
of the Jews, including Mordecai and Esther (Esther 3)

Haman said to King Ahasuerus, "There is a certain unassimilated
nation scattered among the other nations throughout the provinces of
your realm; their laws are different from those of all the other
nations, and the royal laws they ignore; hence it is not in the king's
interests to tolerate them. If their destruction be signed, so please the
king, I am ready to pay ten thousand talents of silver..." (Est 3:8-9).

"Keep the money," [King Ahasuerus] said, "and you can have the
people too; do what you like with them" (Est 3:11).

Mordecai and Esther move to avert the disaster (Esther 4)

When Mordecai learned what had happened, he tore his garments and put on sackcloth and ashes... (Est 4:1).

When Queen Esther's maids and eunuchs came and told her, she was overcome with grief... (Est 4:4).

Mordecai sends the death edict to Esther

[Mordecai] also gave [Hathach] a copy of the edict of extermination published in Susa for him to show Esther for her information, with the message that she was to go to the king and implore his favour and plead with him for the race to which she belonged.... [She was to] invoke the Lord, speak to the king for [the Jews] and save [the Jews] from death! (Est 4:8-8b)

Esther, by approaching the king without invitation, invites death

Whereupon Esther sent this reply to Mordecai, "Go and assemble all the Jews now in Susa and fast for me. Do not eat or drink day or night for three days. For my part, I and my waiting women shall keep the same fast, after which I shall go to the king in spite of the law; and if I perish, I perish" (Est 4:15-16).

Esther's Prayer

"I have been *taught from infancy*
in the bosom of my family
that you, Lord, have chosen
Israel out of all the nations
and our ancestors out of all before them,
to be your heritage for ever;
and that you have treated them as you promised"
(Est 4:17m, emphasis mine).

Esther makes her plea to the king (Esther 7)

"If I have found favour in your eyes, O king," Queen Esther replied, "and if it please your majesty, grant me my life—that is my request; and the lives of my people—that is what I want. For we have been handed over, my people and I, to destruction, slaughter and annihilation..." (Est 7:3-4).

The king grants Esther's wishes; Haman is hanged for his treachery (Esther 8)

That same day King Ahasuerus gave Queen Esther the house of Haman the persecutor of the Jews. Mordecai was presented to the king, Esther having revealed their mutual relationship. The king had recovered his signet ring from Haman, took it off and gave it to Mordecai, while Esther gave Mordecai charge of Haman's house (Est 8:1-2).

Mordecai grows in power and fame (Esther 9)

And indeed Mordecai was a power in the palace, and his fame was spreading through all the provinces; Mordecai was steadily growing more powerful (Est 9:4).

The father-daughter team of Mordecai and Esther faced danger together. The villain was slain. The people of Israel were saved. Mordecai and Esther came out on top. A bit dramatic perhaps, but the principles are there. Mordecai was a *knowing* father. Esther had been properly taught from her youth. When the chips were down she was willing to pay the price, even if it meant her life, in obedience to God and her stepfather.

Two Bible stories from the Old Testament—which do you most identify with?

Most of us are a little of both. Our children, however, desperately need us to be their "Mordecai" today—a *velvet and steel, knowing* guide to help them develop into the adult God plans for them to be.

How do we gain essential knowledge about our children? What areas of their lives do we need to know about firsthand? Secondhand stories are just not good enough for men of *velvet and steel.*

We should first understand that when God made us and the world around us, he was careful to fill this world with "one-of-a-kind." Every snowflake, each leaf, each mountain, each animal, and every human from the beginning of time has been fashioned to be unique and individual.

Each of our children, while created in the image and likeness of God, is one-of-a-kind. No two look exactly alike, act alike, talk alike, think alike, or develop at the same rate of speed or in the same manner. How fascinating and wonderful that we can all be children of the one God and yet still be so different from one another! Could our uniqueness be part of God's plan and desire for a personal and individual relationship with each of us? I believe so. We are invited into a union with God that is like no other. We are, each one of us, called to be one with him (see Jn 17:21).

Fathers, therefore, are to know each child also as an individual, each with strengths and weaknesses of his/her own. No two youngsters, even from the same family and background, can be viewed in exactly the same way. With that reality firmly in mind, what are the most important general areas that we, as *knowing* fathers, should become thoroughly familiar with?

Physical Development

Every child is *just right*; not perfect, just right! Some are large, some are small, some are tall, some are short, some are thin, some are ample—not perfect, just right. There are children who are light on their feet, agile, and coordinated, while others find it difficult to navigate a hallway. Some boys and girls are physically gifted. They are talented in the area of sports. That's great! They can be encouraged to work and develop those gifts.

Most of our children are what I would call physical education material, not really talented enough to make the varsity but they can still benefit and have fun from little league type activities. Then there are those who just can't hit or catch a ball, score a goal or catch a pass. Not perfect but *just right* for them.

I remember those times at PE when the coach would make us choose up teams. Two captains would be selected and the rest of us would gather in a group while the captains alternately picked team members one by one. This has to be one of man's most barbaric processes! I can still remember the looks on the faces of the boys who were always among the last to be chosen. They stood alone on the field as the selection came down to the last few players. It was clear that neither team really wanted them. Their eyes were downcast as they prayed for the selection process to be over, just hoping that they wouldn't be the very last to be picked. I'm sure they dreaded PE for they knew that in their teammates' eyes they didn't quite measure up. Is it any wonder that self-esteem is a major problem for today's youth?

Whether your children are varsity material or not, knowing their physical capacity can help you develop plans to insure their good self-image.

My wife expressed best what it was like to be chosen last and how important a role a father can play in bringing his son—or daughter—back from the clutches of rejection.

"Chosen"

Children at play
On a warm summer's day,
Choosing up sides for a game...
Hearts beating fast,

"Don't let me be last,
Oh, please let them call my name!"

Remember the fear
As you waited to hear
If you would be wanted or not.
It's quite natural to care,
Some even despair,
Acceptance like love means a lot.

We each need to know
That wherever we go,
Whatever we do say or think...
There'll be someone to say,
"Hey, pal, you're okay,"
With a word, or a smile, or a wink.

And if you're lucky like me,
There is one you see,
One who waits with arms open wide.
He says, "Come as you are,
You won't have to go far,
To feel safe and secure by my side."

He calls me by name
Makes me glad that I came
His eyes tell me I'm Number One.
With him to protect me
Let others reject me.
He's my Dad! I'm so glad I'm his son!

What a terrific relationship for a son to have with his father! That son will never doubt how special he is. Even though others may deride him, he knows that in dad's eyes he's the best there is.

Fathers also, however, need to know about the physical development of their daughters. Although sports can be just as important to girls as they are to boys, there are other areas where dad can play an important supporting role. He needs to be aware of what she is going through as she becomes a young woman. When those hormones kick in, you may hardly recognize the little girl who used to crawl up onto your lap and fall asleep as you read to her. The advice I received from my wife and daughters was that, at those times, they need to be loved and accepted just as they are, mood swings and all. It was not the time for a father-daughter sermon.

Your children mature at their own rate of speed. A dad needs to know where his children are physically at *all* stages of their lives. We can't place expectations upon our kids that are too great, especially in the area of sports or even chores around the house. A seven-year-old should not be expected to do what his twelve-year-old brother can do. We need to know the physical capacity of each of our children. And just as important, we dads need to be aware that it is vitally important to our children to be physically acceptable to their peers. Knowing how to help each child accept his/her looks, physical abilities, and limitations and feel good about who he/she is, will help him/her weather the storms of growing up.

Mental Development

I never really learned to read properly. To this very day, unless I have previously heard a word pronounced, I can't sound it out. Nor can I spell a word unless I have first committed it to memory. Testing has confirmed that my IQ is sufficient and that I never should have had a major problem. However, if I had been evaluated as a child, my teachers would probably have found that I had some sort of learning disability.

My mother and step-father were both educators. It could reasonably have been expected then that my problem should have been identified early, enabling me to receive the help I needed. I'm not sure if they ever really knew how much I struggled in school. We never discussed it. It just wasn't a topic of conversation. I'm certain that my mother's long battle with cancer commanded most of their attention. But much of my pain could possibly have been averted if I just knew that my parents understood and were willing to take an active part in my development.

The problems I experienced all through school led me to make sure that I would be a positive influence in my own children's mental development. I wanted to be part of the solution, not part of the problem. In order to be an encourager and a supporter, I needed to know each child's intellectual strengths and weaknesses—their mental capacity.

Our first daughter, Laura, began to speak at a very early age. She had memorized "The Night Before Christmas" poem before she was two years old. Math, however, has always been a struggle for her. Her talents lie in the fields of home economics, gardening, music, and other areas of creativity. Her mother and I learned early to praise Laura's strong suits and gently help her in the areas where she was not as gifted. As a result of our relationship with her and her own personal relationship with the Lord, Laura has blossomed into a respected leader in her church. She is part of the music ministry there as well as a mentor to hurting women.

Lisa, our second child, is a talented, loving, caring registered nurse—a knowledgeable, highly skilled professional. She has the reputation of being a *mover and a shaker*, but finishing nursing school was a challenge for her. She pushed herself through long hours of study. My role was that of an encourager, for I knew she could do it. Her mother and I were there to provide a lovingly administered push when her spirits were low.

Every child is just right; not perfect, just right!

Our son, Kevin, now a civil engineer, was, in his growing up years, always mentally ahead of his physical abilities. He could picture a tree fort in his mind and yet, as a child, he had not developed the building skills necessary to always make it happen. Often his projects would be a source of frustration instead of satisfaction. Through his own perseverance and our encouragement, Kevin is now building hospitals instead of tree forts. When his son, Chris, occasionally needs help with a building project, he is fortunate to have a dad quite qualified to do the job.

Our youngest daughter, Lynda, was probably our most well-rounded student. By the time she came along we were able to afford better schooling for her. She wasn't a whiz kid, but she was a hard worker, and her name could usually be found on the honor roll. Today Lynda excels in her work as a physical therapist and just recently has found even greater fulfillment as a new wife and mother.

Four children, each a bit different, none of them perfect—all just right. The one thing they each had in common was their desire to learn. As teenagers, they also seemed to develop decent work habits, which have stood them in good stead to this day. Now as parents themselves we can see their determination to pass on these good habits to their own children.

Every child is an individual and as such, requires individual support and assistance tailored to his/her needs.

For several years, I was an active board member of a school for special children, the majority with Down syndrome. When a child with Down syndrome is born, most parents experience feelings of overwhelming shock and disbelief. They search for support and advice. Life will never again be the same. What I came to understand was that each child could be helped. In a number of cases the individual can learn to live an active, fulfilling life. Children who, at birth, had not been expected to be able to function independently, often surprise their parents and even the staff of the school. Loving attention, persistent effort, and teamwork between the parents, grandparents, and staff accomplish near miracles.

Where are your children mentally? Do you know what their mental capacity is? Not every child will make the honor roll. So what! Some of the brightest stars of industry, politics, and/or science never succeeded scholastically. Our job is to know the proper pace to set for our children to help them reach *their highest* potential.

Emotional Development

I can't begin to count the number of times I have relived a personal encounter—an encounter in which I have spoken emotionally without properly weighing how the words might come across. I often won the battle but at the risk of losing the war. I lacked tact and sensitivity in dealing with others. My only goal was to make my point.

No one enjoys, or can properly profit from, abrupt or insensitive remarks. A combination of wisdom and skill, tactfully communicated, will very often spell the difference between success or failure in life's relationships.

There are no real problems in life—just people. Getting along with others is a vital skill for us, as fathers, to pass on to our children.

When our children were young I encouraged the playing of board games. I felt that an evening of Monopoly would give all of us an opportunity to compete and have fun. It also gave me the chance to watch the children in both winning and losing situations. How our kids reacted gave me firsthand information on how they were maturing. When the kids reached an age when they could understand the finer points of the game, I no longer helped them or allowed them to replay mistakes.

I probably should have been more of a *velvet* man as I look back, but I did have their best interests at heart, although my wife and children might disagree. Rita tells me that the children would run crying to her because they did not want to spend more quality time with their father—mainly because I wouldn't let them win. So don't be afraid to let those "fun" times be fun times. We all have to win sometime, therefore make sure the kids know the joy of winning as well as how to handle the disappointment of losing.

It is interesting that as adults now, our kids all gain a measure, *or perhaps a lot*, of satisfaction from beating their dad at everything from golf to gardening. It's their time to shine!

Where are your children emotionally? Find out by watching, listening, and asking questions. How do they handle adversity, success, winning, or losing? Do they get along with peers, playmates, teachers, and siblings? Are they bullies or do they help those who are weaker? Are they gentle with pets and small animals? Are they angry or calm in most situations? Every day can be a window into your children's emotional development. *Know* them well.

Spiritual Development

Young children are open and will accept their parents' and/or teachers' concept of God. As they move up in years and observe how the world often says one thing only to practice something very different, they can lose their faith.

I ran across a story by Dan Millman I'd like to share with you (*Sacred Journey of the Peaceful Warrior*, H. J. Kramer, Inc., 1991). It talks about children's spiritual development.

> Soon after her brother was born, little Sachi began to ask her parents to leave her alone with the new baby. They worried that like most four-year-olds, she might feel jealous and want to hit or shake him, so they said no. But she showed no signs of jealousy. She treated the baby with kindness and her pleas to be left alone with him became more urgent. They decided to allow it.
>
> Elated, she went into the baby's room and shut the door, but it opened a crack—enough for her curious parents to peek in and listen. They saw little Sachi walk quietly up to her baby brother, put her face close to his and say quietly, "Baby, tell me what God feels like. I'm starting to forget."

In the first chapter of Jeremiah, God speaks to him, and to all of us, saying, "Before I formed you in the womb, I *knew* you…" (Jr 1:5, emphasis mine). Just as little Sachi began to forget about God, our own children will start to forget and to question. Is there really a loving God? Is Jesus his Son? Does God have a unique plan for my life? Is the Bible really God's textbook for living? When I'm bad, can I be forgiven? How can God love me when I'm so unlovable? Are Grandma and Grandpa together in heaven? Why did my pet hamster have to die? These are all questions that our children may ask as their faith matures.

By knowing where your children are spiritually, you can anticipate their questions before they arise and have your answers ready. A father who knows his children will be prepared to talk on each child's level and give honest and satisfying answers to their questions of faith.

Mordecai *knew* Esther. We read that he taught her from her youth. When the test came, they both passed. We can be assured that our tests will also come. The time to plan for the future is now. The time to reach our children is when they are young. Fathers, know your children. Know them physically, mentally, emotionally, and spiritually. Don't chance losing them to the world.

Discussion Questions

1. Are you a "knowing" father?

2. Do you most resemble Eli or Mordecai?

3. How can you learn more about each of your children?

4. As a knowing father, do you need to make changes in your approaches to your children?

5. Which of these areas could use your immediate attention?

Child's Name	Physical	Mental	Emotional	Spiritual

6. What are your action plans?

7. Are you and your wife in agreement concerning your plans?

6

It's a Team Effort

The first chapter of this book speaks about the crisis that parents face today. Dads and moms are clearly outnumbered. We are up against a world which operates under a different set of values and rules. A "me first" mentality infects our environment. If families are to survive and prosper, they need all the help they can get.

Our neighborhood was a mixture of Irish Catholic and Jewish families. The houses and flats were small and bunched together, but each had a front porch where neighbors gathered in the evening. It was a melting pot of different cultures and religions but all believed in "family." I had several dozen surrogate grandparents, aunts, and uncles all ready to scold me or to report any misbehavior to my mother and stepfather. But they were also available to protect me from the neighborhood bully or from any intruder. Mother felt safe and secure in allowing me to continue to play after dark, for my neighborhood "family" was always there, watching out for me.

It is unfortunate that we can't return to the that era. My old neighborhood is now a ghetto of abandoned buildings. No one lives there these days, but if they did, there would probably be bars on the windows.

I now live in South Florida, on a cul-de-sac in a suburban community. There are a dozen families living within a hundred yards of one another. Rita and I know five of them by sight but have only been invited into one of their homes. There are no front porches. We rarely speak. Each of us is busy with many things going in different directions. How sad that neighbors, for the most part, have lost the inclination to reach out and touch one another!

Not only are our neighborhoods very different from those of the past, but our society has become very mobile. In our own family we have members scattered from coast to coast. Our daughters Laura and Lisa and their families live in our old hometown of St. Louis, Missouri. Kevin and his family reside in northern Florida, 250 miles from us. And Lynda, our youngest, along with her husband and baby live in Bakersfield, California. Our extended family is even more widely disbursed. This situation is not unique. Unfortunately, our family probably mirrors most families of this day and age.

Although the world around us is very different now, and building a team of partners in your children's development may be a challenge, it can be done.

It's not easy, but your children deserve a mother-father team they can count on.

Communication with our spouses is vital and it is a decision that we each must make. However, that is only half the formula to a successful parenting partnership. The other half is being able to understand who we are and who our spouse is. We need to realize that how each of us feels and acts comes from our own unique set of life experiences. This understanding, then, forms the basis for compromise and agreement. Fathers often share about how difficult it is for them and their wives to reach agreement. Each has a different point of reference when it comes to child-rearing. The establishing of discipline, privileges, household chores, eating habits, and the like all present a challenge to today's couple. It's not easy, but your children deserve a mother-father team they can count on.

Although our children want and need order and consistency in their lives, they will, from time to time, try us on for size. Even from a very early age, children will endeavor to get their own way if at all possible. If one parent is steadfast they will often seek out the other, looking for an opening. It takes a team effort.

I remember an incident that took place at a church service a few years ago. In the pew just ahead of us was a young couple with two beautiful little girls. One daughter was about five and the other looked to be about three.

The three-year-old, sitting close to her mother, was mildly misbehaving, climbing up and down on the seat—nothing major, just a local disturbance.

The mother, however, would have none of it. She took her young daughter onto her lap, looked straight into her eyes, and then spoke softly into her ear. The child's reaction was immediate. She was miffed to say the least. She pulled away from her mother and moved across the pew to her father, looking back at Mom over her shoulder as she went. That look showed pure defiance. It also conveyed the message, "If I can't get my way with you, Mom, I'll try Dad."

Dad, who had been absorbed in the service, was oblivious to the interaction that had taken place between mother and daughter. The three-year-old climbed up on Dad's lap, put her arms around his neck, kissed him and softly rubbed her little cheek against his—already a femme-fatale at three years of age. She then looked over at her mother with a satisfied expression on her face that said all too clearly, "I've won, Mom. I've found a way around you." I'm sure those parents will have their hands full, in the future, with that little one.

If you and your wife don't communicate, if you don't take time to understand each other and agree on a team approach, your children will sense that weakness and push an ever-growing wedge between you. In that kind of situation, everybody loses! Your marriage won't be all it can be and your children will lose the benefits of growing up in a home that exemplifies God's order for couples. That model is given to us in Genesis 2:24: "…a man leaves his father and mother and becomes attached to his wife, and they become *one* flesh." A united couple is the cornerstone of a well-functioning family.

A united couple is the cornerstone of a well-functioning family.

Just as a cornerstone is not the whole building, however, our children require a diverse but complimentary set of teachers and role models in order to become the well-rounded individuals they are meant to be.

Grandparents can be key members of your team. They already adore their grandchildren and can be positive examples for your children to emulate. At times their influence can be even more effective than that of the parents. Youngsters will often listen to a message delivered by a wise grandma or grandpa that they might otherwise reject if that same message were given by their parents.

Our grandchildren, Josh and Jessi, recently visited us in South Florida. Since Joshua, fifteen, was fast approaching driving age, and Jessi, thirteen, wasn't far behind, I saw a golden opportunity.

Our community had recently been shaken by a terrible tragedy. A sixteen-year-old girl, who had just secured her driver's license, had taken a Sunday evening joy-ride. She and her younger brother had picked up four friends and had headed down a lonely stretch of road toward the Everglades. Her speed had later been estimated at more than eighty-five miles an hour. She lost control of the car and plunged into a nearby canal. The vehicle quickly sank and four of the young people were drowned.

Our community and the local high school where the four attended went into deep mourning. As the holidays approached, the site of the accident was decorated with crosses, graffiti, and a Christmas tree. I visited the site, which is only about fifteen minutes from our home. It had a powerful impact on me and I made a mental note that perhaps some good could come from the tragedy if it could help to make some important points about driving to Josh and Jessi.

Grandparents can be key members of your team.

During their visit the following summer, the three of us took a trip to the site. The crosses had weathered, the barren Christmas tree looked dreary and forlorn, but the fading graffiti was still heart-wrenching. I explained the details surrounding the accident to the kids—how young and inexperienced the driver was, how excess speed is an open invitation to disaster, and how extreme care should be taken when driving at night, especially in unlighted and unfamiliar areas.

The three of us discussed the lack of judgment, not only by the driver but by her fellow passengers as well. I told them that if they ever found themselves in a similar situation, they were to demand to be let out of the car immediately, seek out the nearest telephone, and call for assistance.

What a perfect opening that was to reinforce a key value of maturity to Josh and Jessi through a real life experience. Both of them would soon be driving. My prayer was that the hour I spent with them left its mark. Hopefully, they learned that there is no substitute for good judgment when they get behind the wheel of a car.

Yes, grandparents can be invaluable members of your team. But in order to be so, they, too, need to know where their grandchildren are physically, mentally, emotionally, and spiritually. You can help them gain that knowledge. Share your plans with them; enlist their input and comments. Make it a joint endeavor. Tell your parents that instead of simply playing Santa Claus and spoiling the youngsters, you want them to become actively involved in the upbringing of their grandchildren. A grandparent's wisdom can be a valuable tool in rearing your kids.

Of course every grandparent isn't equipped to be a mentor. As parents, you and your wife need to evaluate each person you invite to come on board as a member of your team. When it comes to your kids, you want to enlist the best for them.

Even if your children's grandparents live hundreds of miles away, they can still be an important part of your team. During each visit we take the time to speak with our children and review each grandchild individually. We ask if there are any areas of need and how we can be of support. We want to present a solid front, united with their parents, committed to the communication of Christian values. Each visit is an opportunity not only for fun and fellowship but also for the sharing and transferring of vital ideas and lessons.

To raise our children right, we need a team effort.

Although our time with our grandchildren is relatively limited, there are other ways of becoming involved. The telephone, fax, e-mail, and regular mail can all be opportunities for sharing.

Rita has been putting out a monthly family newsletter, which she does on the computer, for the past three years. *Mema's Memo* has become a fun way of communicating with family, extended family, and close friends. There are various articles such as Papa's Place, Rita's Recipe Report, Birthdays of the Month, Focus on Family and Friends, and Letters to the Editor. Now that we have acquired a scanner, Rita also puts in one or two picture pages a month, which have become a big hit. Perhaps most importantly, however, is that there is always room to print an article about a grandchild's particular achievement, award, or maybe just something special to build up a little one who might be feeling left out. For the most part the newsletter is positive and uplifting. Rita tries hard not to print anything negative unless there might be a need for concentrated prayer in a certain area. The *Memo* has become a way of reaching across the miles and helping us get to know one another better while affording a perfect place to share values and perhaps even a word or two of wisdom when appropriate.

At last count the circulation of the newsletter was forty-four copies a month. *Mema's Memo* is sent not only to our children and grandchildren but also to nieces, nephews, cousins, and other extended family and friends living in at least ten different states. A cousin from New Orleans recently wrote: "Keep those *Memos* coming; they are the binding force that keeps family together regardless of the miles that separate us." In a phone conversation with our daughter Laura, Rita asked her how she viewed the newsletter. Laura replied, "I'm standing in my kitchen as we speak, Mom, and when you asked that question my eyes fell on an old 1940's style apron that I have on display.

The *Memo* is like those apron strings. It ties us together, and though it isn't just about you, we get to see things through your eyes."

I think my wife has hit upon a most unique and interesting way of communicating with those we love. And I know that she would feel honored if you would like to implement the newsletter idea into your own family. We've discovered that everybody we know loves to see their name in print!

We can never lower the standard.

The written word is one form of communication; another is the telephone. Recently, Angie (nine years old), was struggling with a difficult math problem. Since numbers have always been one of my strengths, Lisa, her mom, called me for help with the problem. After a quick review I called back and took Angie through the solution step by step. Not a big deal to me, but to Angie it was. I want all the grandchildren to know that grandpa is available any time of the day or night, whenever they might need him.

Grandparents can play a major role in any or all of life's events. Births, the first day of school, athletic events, school plays, recitals, first communion, confirmation, graduation, prom nights, and of course weddings, can all be extra special events if dads and moms will plan ahead and seek interaction and input from the children's grandparents.

Our granddaughter, Jessi, is thirteen going on twenty. Grandma Rita has already made plans, and has okayed it with Jessi's mother, to take her off by herself for a time as soon as she begins those monthly cycles that usher her into puberty. Rita wants that to be a special time for Jessi—a time of approval and affirmation for the young woman that she is about to become. She wants the two of them to have fun shopping, going to a show and out for dinner, and maybe even having a makeover to celebrate the new Jessi. But even more important, Rita wants that time to share some of the truths she has gleaned over the years about what it means to be a Christian woman. Truths she hopes will help Jessi through those difficult teen years when peer pressure is at its worst. Besides sharing some of her own teenage experiences, one thing Rita plans to do is take Chapter 31 from Proverbs and put it into the language of today. What a precious memory that time together will be for each of them.

And don't forget about aunts and uncles when you're making up your team. They each have unique experiences to share. The larger your team, the wider the scope and the richer the message.

Rita's sister, Lois, became a trusted confidante to each of our daughters in turn. Our girls always knew they had someone who would be there for them.

Lois was a great listener but would give advice if it was requested. I am certain that our kids had confidential talks with Lois that Rita and I will never know about. How important that those times be shared with a team member whose judgment you trust.

Now, many years later, I am pleased to learn that each of our daughters in St. Louis has followed the lead of their Aunt Lois and has made herself available to her nieces and nephews in just the same way. The children know that if they have a problem that they would rather discuss with someone other than their parents, they can always turn to their Aunt Laura or Aunt Lisa. Each has promised her availability should the need ever arise.

Cousins, too, often have skills and expertise to share. Our niece, Karen, has used her skills in career counseling to help her cousins make plans for their education. Elizabeth, another niece, is a young doctor who has agreed to help our granddaughter, Jessi, determine if medicine is really the career that she wants to pursue.

Siblings, both older and younger, can also help. A troubled young man we know has a dedicated younger sister who can often reach him when his parents cannot.

Dear friends of ours, the Neffs, have a daughter, Sarah, who was married recently. She and her new spouse have agreed to share the rationale and process they took in arriving at their decisions concerning pre-marital sexual purity.

Sarah's Story by Chuck Neff (Sarah's dad)

The pile of personal papers included old bank ledgers, copies of social security applications for our children, and even an old U.S. Savings Bond. Except for the savings bond, the file was filled with a lot of "stuff" I didn't need anymore. I found myself shaking my head in mock disbelief that I had ever considered any of this worth saving in the first place.

As I waded through the maze of documents, the edge of an old letter seemed to be peeking out from under the sea of vintage records. The letter was addressed to me and it was from our oldest daughter, Sarah. The postmark told me it had been written five years ago while she was a freshman in college.

I had always saved the special letters from our children, but what was this one, I wondered. Why had I stowed this one away? I took the letter out of the envelope, unfolded it and began to read:

"Dear Dad,
    I just wanted to let you know that I love you very much. I really love

being able to talk to you and Mom about things like sex—things that some kids would not dream about even mentioning in front of their parents. You guys are really the greatest. I know you trust me and I would never betray that trust. It's too important to me."

Sure, now I remembered. The "how-about-if-my-boyfriend-spends-the-weekend-at-my-college-apartment" letter!

Sarah had been dating her boyfriend for about a year. She had gone back to college for her sophomore year and wanted Mark not only to come up for a weekend but also to stay at her apartment. Needless to say, my wife, Judy, and I were not crazy about the idea. Permitting (and ostensibly condoning) young adults to stray into that kind of situation is a troublesome venture. But Sarah assured us that Mark would sleep on the couch and that "nothing would happen."

One of the things we had preached for years in our family was trust. We had tried to instill a sense of honesty in our children. If we could be honest with one another and trust each other in the little things, then we could be honest and trust each other with the big things…like sex.

My wife and I have four children. Sarah is our oldest. I remember telling her one time that whether she liked it or not, she would always be a role model to her brother and sisters. She did not like hearing that. I could tell by the way she huffed out of the room, looked back and said in a rather loud voice that that wasn't fair.

For me as a father, the one area which had always been the most difficult (and frightening) to deal with was sex. Trying to combat that worldly onslaught is a tiresome, frustrating fight that I have wondered at times if it were possible to win.

If we have had any success with our children in trying to instill values in their lives, it is due in large part to their mother. In many ways Sarah's life has been shaped and molded by Judy's love, wisdom, and faith.

One night during dinner, when Sarah was in her early teens, she asked why it was wrong to have pre-marital sex. Judy paused for only a moment and threw the question right back. "You tell me, Sarah. Why is it wrong to have premarital sex?"

Sarah thought for a moment and said, "Because God says it's wrong." Judy nodded in agreement.

As I recalled that evening so many years ago, I smiled at the little victory we seemed to have gained through that simple exchange between a mother and a daughter. I glanced back at Sarah's letter and continued to read.

"I want you to know that you have nothing to worry about. You and Mom did a wonderful job raising me. You guys should really stop second-guessing yourselves. Your morals and values have been passed down and they are with me—*always*. Mark and I are responsible and we also know what is right and wrong and where that fine line is drawn. He respects me and you. And, so do I.

For all you have done for me, I can only repay you with my love, trust, and respect. Fortunately, you make it easy to give those things to you.

Your open mind and trust in me are wonderful and I love you for it. I just wanted to say that I love you and thank you for trusting me and giving me space to earn that trust.

I love you with all of my heart. Thank you for being the best Dad in the world."

There is a postscript to that letter of five years ago. Sarah and Mark were married in November 1996. All through their courtship and their engagement they vowed to wait until they were married to begin their sexual relationship. What a role model Sarah was for the rest of our family.

A few months before Sarah and Mark were married, Judy was sitting around the kitchen table with our daughters. The subject of sex came up again and this time it was Sarah who imparted the seeds of wisdom to her sisters.

"I know that God tells us it is wrong to be sexually active outside of marriage. I also know that as a twenty-four-year-old woman I can decide to have sex with Mark anytime I want to. But, years ago I promised myself that I would never decide to have sex for the first time in a moment of heated passion. I vowed that I would wait until the next morning and then decide if I wanted to have sex before I was married. We still plan on waiting."

The story reaffirmed my belief that as a family we have to talk openly and often about our family values and that we can never lower the standard in what we believe to be true, no matter what the world seems to be saying to us and to our children. Finally, there is no doubt in my mind that if Judy and I are good parents to our children, it is because of the graces we receive from God to be who he wants us to be and who our children deserve us to be.

> As I think back about the story, I have the lasting impression that our daughter Sarah is, indeed, a precious, precious gift from God. And what a gift she gave back to Judy and me as she reached out to touch and make a difference in the lives of her two sisters.

What a beautiful story. It is certainly right and appropriate for parents to share God's plan for their children concerning sex. But what a powerful message it becomes when an older sister can reinforce that same message in today's language to her younger siblings.

Friends like the Neffs make wonderful members of your team. Rita and I have been blessed with many who live the kind of life we want our children and grandchildren to emulate. The larger your team, the greater the chance that at least one of them will be able to reach your child when he or she has a need.

It is necessary, now, to begin to put together a team of God's people to help with the important responsibility of *raising your children right*—not perfect people (there is no such being), just people who are moving in the right direction. You don't have to go it alone. God has an army of helpers out there for you to choose from. Know your children, develop your plans, build your team. We are in a war for the hearts of our children. To win that war against the pull of the world, we definitely need a team effort.

Discussion Questions

1. Are you and your wife operating as a team? Give some examples.

2. Have the two of you discussed and worked through your family-of-origin differences?

3. Are you both steadfast in your decisions when dealing with the children?

4. Do you have developmental plans for each child and have you shared these plans with their grandparents?

5. Have you asked the grandparents to join your team? Have you explained what part you wish them to play on your team?

6. What about extended family? Have you identified their skill areas?

7. Friends, teachers, pastors—can they play a part in your team effort?

8. Ask God to be a key member of your team.

7

Center Stage

Our grandson, Joshua, recently made his acting debut as the lead in his school play. Josh and the other cast members practiced for weeks to get ready for their performance. There were lines to learn, facial expressions to develop, and body language and gestures to perfect. The cast knew that they were going to be "center stage." They would have the audience's full attention.

Joshua's character, Horace Wilmerding, is a loud, obnoxious old man who enters a hospital for a few days for what he thinks will be a routine physical examination. While there, his foul disposition manages to alienate the entire staff of care-givers. They retaliate by giving him a very potent sedative. During the deep sleep that follows, Horace believes that he has died. He is, however, quite aware of all those who, he thinks, have come to view his remains. As he listens to the comments visitors make about him, Horace is surprised and horrified to learn that even those he loves the most thought him unlovable, to say the least. In the end, a nicer, much changed Horace awakens to find that he has been given an opportunity to change his image before it's too late. Horace Wilmerding was given a second chance. Most of us, as fathers, will never be afforded that same opportunity.

Josh's play makes a couple points and raises a few questions that we might like to take a look at:

1. We are always center stage.

2. Children, *from toddler age on*, are constantly watching Dad.

3. What messages are we delivering?

4. Does our lifestyle reinforce our spoken word?

5. Have we taken the time to repair any damages along the way?

During one of their visits, the two older grandchildren were taking a drive with me. Clipped to my visor was a radar detector. All at once it picked up a signal and began to chirp loudly. Our granddaughter, Jessi, an inquiring soul, asked, "Grandpa, what's that?" Embarrassed, I mumbled something about it helping me to find police assistance when I needed it. What I said was a lie!

We never know when a test might present itself.

The more I thought about it, the more convicted I got. How can a dad, or for that matter, a granddad, preach respect for authority while he blatantly looks for ways to circumvent the law?

That radar detector is gone now. Whether as a dad or a grandfather, I have to live up to the standards I want my offspring to follow. I am not afforded the luxury of cheating on my taxes or lying to my boss, my wife, or anyone else for that matter because that type of behavior sends the message that Dad doesn't practice what he preaches. He asks his children to live up to standards that he, himself, refuses to abide by. We are always on stage. They are always watching.

We never know when a test might present itself. A few years ago I took my old Pontiac back to the dealership for repairs. Rita followed to give me a lift back home. As I drove into the service area I was confronted with three different booths or stations. A service representative was behind each. I gathered from the displays that the service department was having some sort of contest. Each booth displayed a different colored banner—red, white, or blue.

I parked the car and walked up to the red booth. The attendant was busy doing some sort of paper work. He never even looked up or acknowledged my presence. One minute passed, then two. I was less than a foot away from the man and he still refused to greet me.

Having spent the better part of four decades in a service-related industry, this man's rudeness and lack of sensitivity infuriated me. I was just about to let him have a barrage of verbal abuse when a small inner voice told me, "Not today, John." As much as I wanted to let him have it, I moved on to the next counter. The service rep there smiled and welcomed me. We discussed the repair work I wanted done. He took my name, address, and phone number and wrote up the repair order. As he finished, he looked up and commented that I looked familiar. He asked if he knew me from somewhere, and frankly, I couldn't place him. He then asked if I gave parenting seminars. It came out that he had attended a father's seminar a year or so previously at a local church.

Before I left, we had a chance to chat for a few minutes about his family and how important the seminar had been to him.

I recounted the experience to Rita on the drive home. It had to have been the Holy Spirit who saved me that day. What if I had blasted that unprofessional young man? What if I had lowered my behavior to his standards? It certainly would have diluted the message I try hard to convey through my ministry.

Like it or not, we are always center stage. The spotlight is always upon us. If we are going to talk the talk, we have got to walk the walk.

We are always center stage.

I've heard it said that a person who doesn't tell the truth must have an excellent memory or, sooner or later, his lying will catch up with him. We can't live by double standards. We can't be one way when the kids are around and another way when they aren't. The inconsistencies are sure to bleed through. Even though our children will probably never know if we cheat on our taxes or take shortcuts in business, we will know, and our teaching will not ring true. Follow your conscience and make right judgments. If you need a yardstick by which to measure those judgments, the Ten Commandments are still one of the best there is (see Exodus 20). To be a Christian father is a call to excellence. Don't settle for anything less.

That call to excellence means that whether on the mountaintop or in the valley, our lives need to be centered on Jesus Christ. God never promised that Christians would have trouble-free lives. He only promised that he would be with us in the valleys (see Psalm 23). Into every family some rain will fall. How our children see us handle the myriad of daily irritations that beset all of us will go a long way toward properly preparing them for life. As they observe how we manage our temper, repay rudeness with kindness, share household tasks, and handle emergencies, those values and good habits will be molded into the moist clay of their characters.

How we handle adversity is of great interest to our children. It is at those times that we are most likely to be under the microscope. They want to see if our Christian values are going to come through for us or not.

Major illness can consume a family. The lives of its members, including the children, can often be put on hold if we allow it to happen. In May of 1995 I was diagnosed with cancer of the esophagus. Esophageal cancer has a five-year survival rate of less than five percent. Three out of four who suffer from it will die within the first two years. There is no proven successful treatment for this type of cancer.

The evening of the day that we found out about my problem, Rita and I spent several hours talking about how we were going to make this journey a family experience. Although we knew the news would be upsetting to our children and grandchildren, we wanted to make the months that followed as positive as possible. We decided to let the grandchildren know exactly what was happening within their frame of reference. They were entitled to know and, besides, we were counting heavily on their prayer support. The prayers of children are very powerful, you know!

Every day we spend together is an opportunity to make memories.

Rita and I decided that we were going to use the time I had left to pass on whatever wisdom we could to the family. But most of all, we were going to have fun and make memories.

Of course I intended to seek out the best medical help available, but we rested secure in the knowledge that God is in control and that I would not leave this earth one day sooner nor one day later than his plan called for.

Since the evening of that significant talk with Rita, there has been a week-long sailing trip, Rita and I celebrated the birth of our newest granddaughter, Devon Marie, in California, we've hosted a family reunion for forty family and extended family members, and we visited the Grand Canyon. All eighteen of our immediate family celebrated the Christmas of '95 at our home in Florida for one week, and the eighteen of us have also visited the Grand Tetons, Yellowstone National Park, and, recently, the island of Jamaica. Every day we spend together is an opportunity to make memories—to take a quiet walk with a grandchild, to go fishing with my sons, or to watch a sunset with my wife. Those have been special times that have been peaceful beyond understanding and we look forward to many more of them in the future.

When our whole family is together we begin each day with a reading from the Bible, then we have some sharing, and finally end with prayer. The grandchildren sit in a circle and are taught by their parents and grandparents (sometimes we're taught by them). We've learned to tithe not only our money but also our time. God seems to honor that. So far I've outlasted the doctor's predictions. I remain clear of cancer and am asymptomatic.

Like it or not, God has called all husbands, fathers, and grandfathers to be spiritual leaders in their homes. The first impression or image a young child has of God will closely resemble his/her own father. How do your children view God through you? Do they see you at prayer? Do you pray with them and for their future? When our children were still very young, Rita and I began to pray with them for the spouse they might one day marry. Are you into Scripture? Reading Bible stories at bedtime can be a high point of your children's day. And let those children see you daily carrying out the work of Jesus Christ as you become the Christian example you are called to be.

Bill Hybels, pastor of Willow Creek Church in Chicago, shares about his father and the Christian example he set for his children.

He tells of how his dad, a successful businessman, always found time to spend Sundays at home with the family. The mornings were dedicated to church, and then there was

To be a Christian father is a call to excellence.

lunch with the family. Early each Sunday afternoon, however, Bill's dad would steal off for a visit to a home for retarded adult women. He would spend an hour or two holding a prayer service and then would lead that group of special women in their favorite hymns. Hybels later became aware that his dad had made that trip each Sunday for more than twenty-five years.

Bill also recounts the day when Christmas fell on a Sunday. Early in the afternoon, as usual, Bill's dad headed for the door. He looked over his shoulder on that particular day and invited Bill to join him. Although he was pulled to stay at home and play with his new toys, he joined his dad for the trip to the home. When they arrived, Bill helped his father unload a trunk full of presents. Each present was carefully wrapped and each had a card. Bill then joined his dad in the small chapel as he held service for the women. When it was over, Bill stood by the door across from his dad. As the ladies began to leave, he watched as his father stopped each one at the door while he searched the pile of presents until he found the gift he had purchased for that particular lady. As he handed her the present he called her by name and then gave each unattractive, untidy, not very clean, but very special lady, a hug. As Bill watched his dad that day and saw the measure of his love for those who were not very lovable, he wanted more than anything in the world to one day be able to walk in his dad's footsteps.

When our own children became teenagers (we had four teens at the same time), I began to wonder in whose footsteps they would follow. I could see them begin to drift this way and that as they tried their wings. About that time

I happened to see a public service announcement. The main character was a young boy about three years old who looked very sad. He sat with his head bowed while the voice-over described the plight of foster children and how they needed homes that offered love and affection if they were to develop properly. As the announcer continued to speak, the little boy slowly raised his head and began to smile. I could not resist the look of hope and anticipation on his little face as that spot ended. I was hooked.

We can't live by double standards.

With all my usual enthusiasm and gusto I approached my wife. But she quickly let me know that although taking in foster children was a great idea, she was the one who would be the primary care-giver. She said she'd have to think and pray about it.

Several months went by and I had almost forgotten the episode. Then, shortly after I arrived home from a business trip, Rita announced that she and the kids had decided that we were going to become a foster family. We made an application to Catholic Charities, went through all the interviews, and finally received our first newborn infant, whom we named Adam.

So began almost four years of joy and a few tears. The day a new baby was to arrive was always filled with excitement and expectation as we wondered what he/she would look like and what kind of temperament he/she would have. Rita inevitably hogged the baby for the first few days, but once she was satisfied that everything was fine, each of us would get our turn. If I had seriously tried to come up with a way of bridging the generation gap, I don't think that I could have found a better way. Our girls would actually vie for the opportunity to hold and care for the baby. They were learning how to handle an infant even before they had one of their own. Our son, too, got into the act and also did his share of nurturing.

Then all too soon the day would come when the case worker would have to pick up "our" baby and take him/her to the new adoptive parents. It didn't matter if the sun was shining those days or not; inside our house it was always raining. Early in the morning each of us would stop by the baby's room for one last kiss and a tearful good-bye. We rested in the knowledge that "our" baby was being taken to a loving home. That didn't make those good-byes any easier, though. We had some of those children, who were always about three days old when we received them, for up to ten months. By that time it really was like giving up our own child.

I don't think you can really understand what love is until you give it away. Rita and I can tell you that work and sacrifice are a small price to pay for the atmosphere that prevailed in our home during those years. And I don't believe we could have picked a better way to give our own children a living example of what Christianity and parenthood are all about.

It is my hope that each of you, along with your wife, will pick an area of service for your family—matching it to your time and talents. Let your kids see Mom and Dad helping others. In fact, better yet, let your children, in their own small way, enter into the process.

The relationship between you and your wife is probably the most important area in which to set the kind of example you want your children to follow. Your daughters will tend to seek spouses who will treat them the way you treat your wife, and your sons will treat their future wives the way they saw you treat their mother. Therefore a loving relationship between the two of you will not only form the solid foundation upon which your children can build their lives, but it will also greatly influence future generations.

Picture, if you will, returning home from a full day's work. You meet your wife in the kitchen and embrace. As you hug, your little one watches from across the room. He laughs, puts down his toys, and runs toward his mom and dad. As he reaches you, he tries to squeeze between your legs. He wants to be right in the middle of that circle of love. Mommy and Daddy's love for one another puts his world in order. All is well.

The scene I've just described may sound a bit corny, even difficult to imagine these days, for it may not happen as often as we would like it to. Unfortunately, the hours in the day are crammed full of work and social activities that just don't leave enough time for the important people in our lives. Our children deserve the best. They deserve a mom and dad who love each other and who take the time to show it. They deserve that peaceful, loving environment in which to grow and develop to their highest potential.

Today's after-school activities are geared more toward outside rather than inside the home, e.g., sports, gymnastics, music or dance lessons, and the like. While these all help to round out children's personalities, they cannot take the place of those one-on-one times with their parents. Those are probably the most important times in your child's life for molding character and setting values. You and your wife are charged with the splendid burden of making your home the warmest, most loving, most interesting, most comfortable, most fun place to be—so that the outside world pales by comparison. It's a tall order and nothing less than your best efforts will make it happen!

While we strive to present a positive role model for our children, it is inevitable that we will make mistakes. There will be times when we hurt feelings without meaning to do so. There will be misunderstandings and promises that we've failed or been unable to keep. If we know we've goofed, it is relatively easy to remedy the situation. A hug and a sincere "I'm sorry, please forgive me" will go a long way toward repairing most of the damage.

It is good to frequently offset hurts before they can take root and do harm. Love notes, flowers, and dates with Dad can make a daughter feel like a princess. And any son's day is brightened by going to a sporting event or just out for a hamburger with Dad. Hurts can become scars all too quickly. Mend them while they're small. The secret is to use preventive measures and make frequent repairs.

There may be times, however, when we don't even realize that we've stepped on somebody's toes—times when we've missed that "look," that drop of the eyes, that shrug of the shoulders, or any of those signs that should clue us to the fact that we've inflicted pain. Put a stop to that pain while it is small. Don't allow it to fester and grow out of proportion.

About every six months, or whenever the atmosphere in our home prompted me, I would call for a family meeting. A few days prior to the event, I would ask all the children and Rita to plan on spending a particular evening with just our family. I asked them to pray and think about what they would like to share at that time. If feelings had been hurt, or if we had not been loving to one another, that was the time for forgiveness to take place. On the other hand, I requested that each of us share at least one fond and affirming memory about every member of the family. At first the kids grumbled and complained, thinking it too hard a task to find something good to say about their siblings. But, little by little, as they took on a positive attitude, the atmosphere in our home would begin to change for the better. Those evenings were, without exception, an uplifting time for all of us. Rita and I fondly recall one such occasion when our daughter Lisa, sixteen years old at the time, began to sob as the sharing drew to a close. Asking her if she was troubled about something, Lisa just cried harder and said, "No, I just feel completely loved!"

Another time, after I had already talked about the positive times that had blessed me with Rita and the kids, I asked the family's forgiveness for any time I had been thoughtless, broken a promise, or hadn't been the kind of father they expected me to be. That's when Lynda began to cry. When I asked her to explain, she reminded me that I had always been faithful in supporting our family's little league activities. Even though I traveled a great deal, I would rearrange my schedule to be there for Kevin's soccer or Lisa's softball games. Then Lynda went on to say, "But, Daddy, you never attended my school's basketball games when I was a cheerleader."

I vividly remember that evening and how embarrassed I was. Lynda wasn't actually playing basketball so I didn't think I needed to be there to cheer her on. She was, however, representing her school and her team, just the same.

My youngest daughter had been performing as a cheerleader and I hadn't even bothered to be there to let her know how proud I was of her. She had carried that hurt around for more than a year and I hadn't even been aware of it.

I told Lynda how sorry I was and how thoughtless I had been. Through our tears we hugged as I asked her forgiveness. The healing process had begun.

That healing might never have taken place, however, if we had not provided the opportunity to make it happen. It is important to test the waters often. When the sea begins to get a little rough—when the atmosphere in your home begins to get a little tense—you know it's time to get your family together for a time of healing, affirming, and forgiving. You never know when it just might be a little too late.

A case in point comes to mind concerning my wife's family. Rita has three younger sisters, Susan, Lois, and Terry. Recently, Rita, Lois, Terry, and I were taking a day-long drive to a Christian conference. As we drove along, the ladies began to share memories of their father.

Lester Lott, a hard-working husband and father of five, died of a heart attack in 1953 at the early age of forty-eight. Rita, the oldest, was sixteen when he died. She loved him deeply. He was not only her father, he was also her best friend. She recalled how he was always there for her, taking her places or helping her with homework. And she remembered the comfort of being able to crawl up on his lap when she was little. He had a way of calming her fears and making everything right again.

Lois was ten when her father died. She remembers how guilty she would feel at times because she wasn't all that sorry he was gone. Her image of her dad was that of a stern taskmaster. Their biggest confrontations would take place at the dinner table when Lois would refuse to eat the food that was set before her. An inevitable clash of wills would occur and her father would make her sit there for what seemed like hours. Looking back now, Lois sees that she and her father were probably very much alike. But at that time he was just someone bigger and stronger than she was, forcing her to bend to his will.

Terry, who was seven when Les died, recalls that her most vivid memory of her father took place when she was four years old. She was playing outside with some friends when her dad called to her from the front porch. She recalled that, as she approached him, he seemed to be smiling. But then when she got close enough he grabbed her and gave her a spanking. To this day, she's not sure why. She only remembers how betrayed she felt.

How sad that that memory is the first thing that comes to mind when Terry thinks of her dad. And isn't it sad that in the mind of a child, one or two injustices, or perceived injustices, can loom larger than years of positive parenting.

These three sisters had the same father. When he died each remembered him differently. I'm sure that Lester Lott wanted to be the best possible father he could be. He probably never even realized that he was sending such mixed messages to his family.

Please don't take chances where your loved ones are concerned. Be very certain that they understand how important and loved they are even when discipline is necessary.

A father is always center stage, day in, day out, year after year. Make your performance consistently effective. Be the role model that God intends for you to be. And please don't let the curtain come down on your mistakes. Rectify them early and often. Make a positive place in the hearts of your children, and also in their memories.

Discussion Questions

1. How did you handle this week's trials? Think about how your actions looked to your children.

2. Is there a moment or two that you would like to relive?

3. Is there an area with which you are having trouble, e.g., temper, language, relationships, availability?

4. Look at your relationship with your wife through your children's eyes. Ask your wife to comment. Do you have repair work to do?

5. Have you set aside a regular time for family sharing?

6. When was the last time you said you were sorry and meant it?

8

It's the Law
(Setting Standards)

Rita and I have moved several times during our forty years of marriage. First from Missouri to Texas, on to Georgia, back again to Missouri, then to Illinois, and finally to Florida. With each move as we became residents of the new state, we were required to take some sort of written exam before the state authorities would issue us driver's licenses. The laws of each state held that driving an automobile is a privilege. To use that privilege Rita and I were required to understand and obey that state's duly established laws governing the operation of an automobile. It's the law!

Every successful business that I have ever been associated with has had a built-in set of operating procedures. Management understood that each employee needed to know how to handle the many everyday responsibilities that a smooth-running business requires. Those operating instructions communicated their wishes:

1. The operation was described.

2. The employee was shown why the work was important.

3. The employee's role was described in detail.

4. Management followed up to be sure the operation was
   being completed properly.

Schools, scout troops, little leagues, part-time jobs—every conceivable activity our children participate in—are governed by rules, regulations, procedures, and/or routines. In order for them to make it in life, our young people, whether in first grade or college, must *respect authority, understand and obey the rules, and be able to perform as members of a team.*

Unfortunately, most of today's families do not operate the way society does. Parents often run a family without standards, and their kids pay the price for it. When those children hit adult life, whether at school or in the business community, they will be ill-prepared to follow the beat.

Our job as fathers, in partnership with our wives, is to set the standard. How we expect our families to operate and how we define the role of each of its members makes up that standard.

Take the time.

Set the

standard.

Earlier this year, I was visiting the home of our daughter Lisa. She and her husband, Mark, were at work and I was preparing to take their three children out with me to run some errands. Before we left, I suggested to the kids, Angie (nine), Katie (five), and John (four), that we surprise their parents by cleaning up the house. As we walked through the first floor, I made assignments for Angie and Katie. Little John and I then went upstairs and I asked him to clean up his bedroom. I pointed out that the bed needed to be made and his clothes and toys were to be put away.

I watched as John began to make his bed and it quickly became apparent that that chore was still a little beyond his capabilities, so I pitched in and we completed it together. Then one of the girls called me from downstairs, so I left him to finish the other tasks.

After a few minutes I returned to John's room just as he was closing his closet door. The room looked great. The bed was made and the clothes and toys were out of sight. All appeared to be in order—until I opened the door to the closet! All the clothes and toys were in a heap on the closet floor. To John the job was finished—out of sight, out of mind. If you can't see it, don't worry about it. John and I spent the next twenty minutes hanging clothes and finding the proper place for each of his toys. I made a little game out of the exercise, and we had a fun time together. At four, since John couldn't yet read, all my instructions were verbal. We took the time to do it right and we did it together.

Unfortunately, I had to leave the next day and one session is not sufficient to establish a standard. Lisa, Mark, and I discussed it before I left, however, and I agreed to follow up on my next visit. As a member of their team, I'm always ready to help them set and reinforce their family standards.

Children can begin to help around the house earlier than we might think. Rita remembers that our girls began to imitate her dusting, mopping, cooking, and dishwashing when they were only toddlers. Our son loved to take things apart and try to put them back together when he was only two. A wise dad will take advantage of this natural curiosity and begin, at a very early age, to develop the skills that will serve his children later in life. Simple tasks, such as picking up after themselves, can be a starting point. As the children grow older, they will be able to take on increasing responsibilities and the tasks can become more complicated.

With older children, standards can be discussed at family meetings, written down, and amended as needed. Children are like the rest of us—we all want and need order and consistency in our lives. Their message to us is: Just tell me the rules, set the standard for me, be consistent, try to be fair and helpful, but don't let me wiggle out of my responsibilities no matter how hard I try.

We all want and need order in our lives.

When I was about ten, I was required to scrub the kitchen and bathroom floors in our small apartment every Saturday morning. Since scrubbing floors was not very exciting, I sometimes hurried through it. I was not allowed to join my friends at play until the job was finished and finished properly. Before I could call the job complete I had to ask for my stepfather's inspection and okay. He wouldn't let me out the door until I had completed the work to standard. I can still remember the Saturday morning I failed the test twice. Although I whined and cried a bit, Dad would not let me leave until the job was completed properly. I had to meet his standard—it was a Ream family law. I'm sure it was those Saturday morning exercises that helped me adapt to Marine discipline eight years later.

You and your partner need to discuss and formulate a list of family chores. Divide the chores into levels by degree of difficulty and time required to complete. Determine just how you want the job to be done and when. Make your assignments, preferably in list form, instruct the kids, and be sure to make follow-up inspections. As your children master one group of tasks they can graduate to the next level of difficulty. You might even consider giving awards at family gatherings for work well done to make it more positive and fun for the kids. You are preparing those children for life as it really is. Take the time. Set the standard.

Our oldest daughter, Laura, has three children ages nine, thirteen, and fifteen. She has a school-day chore list and a weekend chore list for each of the kids. As the tasks are completed there is a place for the children to check them off. Everything is expected to be completed before bedtime and without having to be reminded. Kitchen cleanup and dishes are the one exception—that chore is to be done right after dinner. Laura says that since the kids know exactly what is expected of them, it has cut down considerably on their fussing and on her always having to keep after them to get things done.

It is good to consider the time element involved when setting your standards. I was required to complete my weekly floor-scrubbing right after breakfast on Saturday morning. My job was to come before anything else that day. I could not put it off until the next day or even that afternoon. The job came first, and my own agenda was second.

Work habits developed now will be invaluable to your children.

Every day, families race to beat the clock. Time is precious. When one family member is late it can throw everybody off. Younger children must understand that getting started on time in the morning is important. Making their bed, brushing their teeth, and getting to the breakfast table on time is significant to every other member of the family. Their promptness or lack thereof can literally make or break a busy family's morning. Consider the stove timer—it can be a good tool with which to begin establishing a morning routine. The method you use is not important. What is vital, however, is that children learn to accept their responsibility as members of your family and that they develop a consideration for everyone else.

As children get older they should be held responsible for getting home in time for the evening meal or for their nighttime curfew. Rita and I required our kids to call if they saw that they could not be home on time. We felt that letting the rest of the family know if we were going to be late was just a common courtesy that responsible people owe to one another. Curfew hours were discussed and set but were not written in stone. There could be exceptions for specific events. And although a curfew was a curfew, we stressed that the kids should call if a problem developed. We did not want them driving irresponsibly just to get home on time.

The ideal, of course, is to decide how your family will function when the children are still small. Train your children to complete their tasks properly and on time. Teach them why learning responsibility is important, not just to them but to the family as a whole. List and describe the jobs they are expected to do. And finally, don't forget to follow-up. You will be wasting your time if you don't make sure that a job is done properly and on time. Work habits developed now will be invaluable to your children as they grow and mature. It is never too late to set family standards. However, with older children, that task may be more difficult. You will undoubtedly meet with resistance, but the results are well worth your effort. Do *not* weaken.

Recently our son, Kevin, and his family spent a few days with us. Our grandson, Chris (seven at the time), and I are both early risers. One morning as I passed his room on the way to the kitchen, I noticed that his bed was not made and his clothes were in a heap on the floor. Not a big deal, but as I passed him in the family room I asked him to please clean up his room while I made us both some breakfast. Chris acknowledged my request but he didn't move. The cartoons on the TV were just too interesting. After a few minutes I reminded him that the bedroom still needed his attention. He replied with an "okay" but his attention was still focused on the TV. Finally I had to get in his face and make sure he understood that when Grandpa asked him to do something he expected him to move and get it done—post haste!

The family should be conditioned to listen and respond without hesitation.

It may seem a bit tough by today's standards—expecting children to carry out requests in a timely fashion—but, call it what you will, instant obedience or first-time response can be more than just a quality trait—it might just save their lives some day.

Located just northwest of Ft. Lauderdale, Florida, is a major highway interchange that is complicated by a north-south railway line. A main through-street which had been under construction crossed the railroad track, and the six-lane road narrowed to a single lane each way.

Some time ago, late in the afternoon when traffic was extremely heavy, westbound traffic had narrowed from three lanes to just one and once you entered the single lane there was no other way to go but straight ahead. A stoplight complicated matters even more, and traffic backed up for several hundred yards.

A gasoline truck had pulled into the single lane and had been caught by the red light as it straddled the railroad track. A line of cars had filled in behind the tanker. Just then a passenger train, moving south, was approaching the crossing blocked by the truck. The traffic could not move and the train could not stop. The rest is history. The train and the truck collided. The truck exploded, killing the driver and several passengers in the surrounding vehicles.

As I visited the site later I thought about the people who had been trapped in their cars. There had been a family of four in a mini-van right behind the tanker. Looking at the scene, I wondered what went through that dad's mind as the train approached. From where he was situated he could see up the track for several hundred yards. He would have had a minute or so to evaluate the situation, make his decision, and communicate it to his family. Did he panic and freeze, or did he give crisp commands that were never carried out? We'll never know for sure. His family didn't make it.

Think for just a moment about what you would have done. What instructions would you have given? Would your family have responded without question or hesitation? As I look back, I'm not sure how my own children would have reacted, but I'm certainly going to make *instant obedience* the topic at a family meeting with our grandchildren.

Children look for their fathers to be the kind of leaders God calls them to be. They need to know they can trust us. So set the standard. Show them the way. Follow up; require that jobs be done properly and on time. When a man of *velvet and steel* speaks, the family should be conditioned to listen and respond without hesitation. Lives—both long- and short-term—are in the balance.

Discussion Questions

1. How does your family operate? Do you have a set of standards?

2. Do you and your wife agree that the family needs a set of operating procedures?

3. If standards are important, when will you make them a priority?

4. Does each family member know what his/her job is and how and when it is to be completed?

5. Do you follow up to see that assignments are finished on time and up to standard?

6. Do your family members, especially grandparents, reinforce your family values?

7. How do you encourage your children to perform to standard? Do you give awards and praise for work well done?

8. Do your children respond to your and your wife's commands the first time? How would they respond in an emergency situation?

9

Training:
Let's Do It Together

Proverbs 22:6 tells us, "Train children in the right way and when old, they will not stray." Footnotes add, "Instruct a child from his earliest years—beginning on his way—according to his dispositions."

To train also means to prepare, to educate, to inform, to pass on in a connected way.

Therefore, God's message to us in Proverbs 22 is to train our children in godly ways to prepare them for the abundant life. We need to pass on wisdom and skills, and we must do so on a continuing basis. It is our job to educate and inform our children and get them ready for adult responsibilities.

Doctor Robert Barnes' book, *Ready for Responsibility* (Zondervan, 1997), stresses preparation for adulthood in two major areas—marriage and work. Fathers are called to implement training processes through which their children can mature into highly responsible adults ready to enter into covenant marriage relationships and prepared to engage in meaningful careers. One additional area of equal importance is that of preparing children for their Christian responsibility of serving others in both church and community. Preparing young people for marriage, work, and service can be a tall order. Where is a dad to look for help?

Let's take a look at the business world, in which training is an absolute necessity. Our bank invested millions of dollars each year in manuals, seminars, and training programs. Our customers expected and demanded competent employees who knew their jobs and who could respond to their needs with skill and sensitivity. All employees spent at least five percent of their time learning more about their job. It was a never-ending process. Even after thirty-seven years in the field, I was still reading and attending classes. We were constantly testing to find the best ways of transferring knowledge.

After experimenting with various video, audio, and self-help methods, how-ever, we most often returned to on-the-job training. We found that a seasoned, mature, patient employee showing a trainee, one-on-one, how an operation was to be performed was the key to our success. While a family and a business differ in many respects, they are also alike. The art of transferring skills and knowledge to our children is one of them.

Get them ready for adult responsibilities.

All of our grandchildren are adequate swimmers. While we are ever watchful and never leave them alone in the water, the children are at home whether in a swimming pool, a lake, or even the ocean. I feel certain that our family could handle almost any water emergency with the confidence that comes from experience and skill. They respect the dangers of swimming and other water sports and are prepared to deal with them. This skill was not taught by reading books on swimming or watching videotapes. Their parents, older cousins, and some-times Grandpa taught them to swim, one-on-one, while in the water with them.

Teacher and student alike had to get wet. The instructor would hold them up and work with them as they learned to float and then swim. As the children gained experience and confidence, the adults would gradually move away but remained close enough to help if needed. Dad, mom, and members of their team taught water skills to their children over time. Because repetition is the mother of learning, we would encourage them to try and try again until they got it right and became confident. Our daughter Lynda is already teaching eighteen-month-old Devon how to feel secure in the water.

Swimming, however, is only one of the many skills we need to transfer. Young children can begin by taking care of themselves and their belongings. Bathing, practicing personal hygiene, attending to their clothing and play-things, plus doing simple household tasks fit well into an initial set of training goals. Then, when you believe they are ready, children can also begin to take on responsibilities that impact others. You might begin with the care of pets.

Our granddaughter, Katie, is five. She is bright and has an infectious laugh. She's a quick learner and always eager to help. Katie is a joy to her parents, Lisa and Mark, and of course to Rita and me. As a gift from one of her cousins, she recently received a baby hamster, which she promptly named Darla. Darla's home is a converted aquarium filled with cedar shavings and equipped with a water bottle, a dish for food, and an assortment of toys. Not a bad place to spend one's life—if you're a hamster. Darla's aquarium is on the floor of a spare bedroom. The door is kept closed because Thomasina, the cat, has been seen casting longing glances in Darla's direction.

I recently spent two weeks with Katie and her family while recuperating from a minor operation. Checking on Darla now and then (her room was across from mine), I noticed that she did not always receive the care she needed. Her dish and water bottle were frequently empty.

Each morning at breakfast I would ask the children if they had taken care of their pets. Angie, the oldest, was responsible for Ginger, their dog, and Thomasina. Darla was, of course, Katie's responsibility, and John had charge of their fish. All would assure me that they had looked after their pets and that all was well.

Repetition is the mother of learning.

One particular morning, however, I happened to look in on Darla and again found the water bottle empty. Since Katie had just assured me of Darla's well being, I called her. I met her at the top of the stairs and we both went in to check on Darla. As I pointed to the empty water bottle Katie was visibly embarrassed. She hurried to fill the bottle with water and added a shot of hamster vitamins. As Katie replaced the water bottle, I suggested that we watch and see if Darla was thirsty. Darla, as you might expect, went right to the bottle and drank without stopping for several minutes—she was, indeed, very thirsty. I watched Katie's face but didn't say anything. Her eyes moistened as she grasped the fact that Darla needed her attention each and every day. When the hamster finished, Katie and I talked about how she was able to get a drink by herself when she was thirsty but that Darla depended on her for almost everything. If Katie forgot, Darla would have to do without.

You might call that a teachable moment. It was an opportunity for Katie to learn a lesson that might help her throughout her lifetime. It has been several weeks now since the above-mentioned incident and Katie's mom reports that Darla has never had to go thirsty again. Katie has assumed her responsibility. Preparing our children for real life is what fathering is all about.

Many successful people did not have an easy time in school. I'm a living example of a reasonably intelligent human being who struggled with schoolwork. I was not taught, nor did I ever develop, the good study habits and routines that are essential to completing work properly and on time. I was constantly waking up to the fact that a major project was due the next day, and I had not even begun to gather the necessary information or materials, let alone think through a plan to finish on time. I needed someone to train and persevere with me to develop those habits. Time and effort invested in me then would have paid hefty dividends for me later.

Our grandchildren are bright and intelligent; however, some will have to work harder than others. Training them to plan their time, develop good study habits, and put first things first are investments in preparing them to meet the challenges of the future.

Training is an investment in preparing children to meet the challenges of the future.

I had to learn the hard way without help or even encouragement. If someone had taken the time to train me, my life would have been immeasurably easier. Family life would certainly be less stressful and more peaceful if we would only take the time to teach our offspring how to function as team members, how to work together, and how to get along with their siblings. Activities like little league, scouting, school, youth groups, and later, marriage and career all present the challenge to compromise and get along with others. These attitudes are best taught early and in the home.

Teaching our children how to prepare a meal, change a flat tire, balance a checkbook, handle credit, maintain the yard, re-light a water heater, how to behave on that first date, paint a wall, do the laundry, clean a bathroom, and shop for a bargain are all skills we need to transfer. Training takes an investment of time, planning, teamwork, and lots of patience. Those attributes did not come easy to me.

Our children would dread family work days, and they had good reason. I often ruined everyone's Thursday evening by announcing a family work project for Saturday morning. Rarely had I planned or thought through the work to be done. Nor did I take the time to explain how I expected the chores to be completed. The work always took much longer than anticipated to finish. No wonder the kids hated the day and I often came away flustered and angry. I often found it easier to do the work myself than to coerce the children into performing properly. Looking back, it's interesting to find that I failed to implement my own tried-and-true business methods. I would have been much more successful if I had taken the time to *communicate what needed to be done, train each of my children in how to do it*, and *encourage them with lots of praise*. And above all I should have thought of ways to *make the job fun*.

Every day presents us with opportunities to train. I'm reminded of two incidents which occurred recently during my stay in St. Louis. Both took place when I invited a family member to join me as I ran some errands.

First let me set the stage concerning incident number one. Our grandson, Josh, was three months away from his sixteenth birthday—that magical day when all teenagers become instant adults. Upon reaching that birthday they can legally be trusted with three thousand pounds of metal commonly referred to as an automobile. Josh had passed his written exam and was armed with a learner's permit. His parents, Laura and Keven, were allowing him to drive under their watchful eye but would make a final decision based upon performance, not his date of birth.

Although Josh believed he was just about ready to drive, he still needed training and experience before assuming responsibility.

On this particular day Josh decided to accompany me on a trip to visit my stepfather, who was ill. As we drove along the busy interstate I pointed out situations that would demand a driver's close attention. There were the usual speeders, drivers weaving in and out of traffic, and those who were obviously impatient, waiting for an opportunity to pass. Just a normal day on the freeway for an accomplished driver, but I saw these as opportunities to share my forty years of experience with my grandson. I asked Josh how he would handle various situations and, for the most part, he gave intelligent, thoughtful answers. However, answering questions and performing under stress can be two entirely different matters. Would he be ready to drive by his sixteenth birthday? Maybe. I was confident though, that his mom and dad were passing on necessary driving skills as they monitored his performance. He would drive when they thought he was ready. Josh and I had a good time in the car that day but I also hope he picked up a few pointers about driving along the way.

The other occasion occurred while Rita and I were visiting her sister, Lois. Lois' son, David, happened to have the day off and I asked if he would like to accompany as I ran a few errands. David, twenty-four, a graduate with honors from the University of Missouri, had recently become a fireman for a city on the outskirts of St. Louis. As we drove we talked about his work. He loves being a fireman like his dad, and he is good at it. Gradually, though, I began to steer our conversation in another direction. Besides fighting fires and being of service to the community in that way, I asked how he was using his talents and treasure to make a difference in the lives of others. David is a committed Christian and so he does understand that he is called to make a difference. He is also an extremely caring individual with much to give. As we talked, a young man whom we both know came to mind and I suggested that perhaps David's friendship and council might truly be of benefit to him.

David hadn't thought much about Christian service, however; his new career had consumed most of his time. As we returned home, David was very thoughtful. I'm sure he was beginning to realize the many gifts he had to share with others, as well as the call for every Christian to do so.

Each of those ordinary car trips became an opportunity to share one-on-one with someone I love. When dads take training seriously, those opportunities are readily available. We need only take the time to look for them. Not just our children and grandchildren will benefit from the skills and values we pass on, but generations to come. What better legacy could we leave?

Discussion Questions

1. Do you and your wife have a training plan for each of your children? Do you have a schedule for implementing that plan?

2. Are you ready for when the next opportunity to train presents itself?

3. Are you in the process of transferring all the skills needed for success in school?

4. Do your children's study habits need help?

5. How well do your children work together?

6. Do each of them perform well when teamwork is required?

7. Do you look for opportunities to be one-on-one with your children/grandchildren?

8. Are you preparing your teens for marriage, career, and Christian service?

10

Looking Ahead

Therefore, everyone who listens to these words of mine and acts on them will be like a sensible man who built his house [family] on rock. Rain came down, floods rose, gales blew and hurled themselves against that house [family], and it did not fall: it was founded on rock. But everyone who listens to these words of mine and does not act on them will be like a *stupid* man who built his house [family] on sand. Rain came down, floods rose, gales blew and struck that house [family], and it fell; and what a fall it had! (Mt 7:24-27, emphasis mine)

The words "house" and "family" are interchangeable here. A modern dictionary definition of "house" is "a family as including kin, ancestors and descendants."

Jesus actually tells us that we are *stupid* if we do not give our family the firm foundation it needs. Build on rock, he says, not sand. Don't risk having your children damaged or even destroyed by the floods and gales of adversity that, sooner or later, will come their way.

A pastor and I were lamenting recently about the sad fact that so many of today's young people seem to move away from the faith in which they were brought up as soon as they move away from their parents' home. At college or in the workplace they are met with overwhelming temptations that they are simply not prepared to deal with. Without the support of their home environment, they all too often embrace the theme that *if it feels good, do it*! We must find a way to provide support and prepare our young people to meet the challenges that they all too soon will face.

As examples of the kind of foresight I'm talking about, let's take a look at a few famous men. Down through the ages these men have been noted for their vision. They had the talent for looking into the future, making plans, and taking steps to prepare those for whom they were responsible.

Lincoln abolished slavery, seeing it as our nation's greatest sin. Franklin D. Roosevelt supported Social Security, looking ahead to the well being of our senior citizens. John F. Kennedy restored pride in our nation through the space program. Pope John XXIII, looking to the future, opened the windows of the Catholic Church and let in the fresh air of the Holy Spirit.

Build on rock, not sand.

What those wise leaders and watchful fathers had in common was foresight. A dad needs to look ahead and know what's coming. He needs to have a plan for whatever might develop. He needs to build his house on rock. I might even say he needs to build his house on *the rock*, which is Jesus.

An early mentor of mine once shared a truth with me that has served me well through the years. He said, "Problems I can handle. It's the surprises that are dangerous." When I fail to look ahead, more often than not I will pay the price for my haste.

At some time or other most of us have purchased an item with the words "Some Assembly Required" printed on the box. In my heart I know that if I would just take the time to read the instructions, I would probably save time in the long run. Now, whether or not it's a "man" thing, I don't know. I only know that once the contents of that box are revealed I seem to have an instant awareness of how it goes together. I reason that I could probably have the whole thing assembled in the time it would take me to read the instructions.

My wife recalls the time we purchased a small two wheeler for one of our grandchildren a couple years ago. I worked on that thing, out in the garage, for several hours while little Angie checked every few minutes to see if I was "done yet." Angie's dad would stroll through the garage every now and then just to see if I might ask him to help. But he told Rita that I said I was doing just fine. Finally Angie ran to her grandmother with the exciting news that Grandpa was finished and he only had three parts left over.

Time is usually the only cost of failing to read instructions. But the cost of failing to understand and prepare for what lies ahead can be immeasurably more dear.

Earlier, I spoke of my two young Haitian friends, Jean, who was eleven and, Gerry, who was ten. They loved to come to our home and play in the pool and then take a long shower. Those things, I'm sure, were not a regular part of their daily routine.

Our home sits on a lake, and our community owns several canoes which can be checked out by residents. One Saturday afternoon, I asked the boys if they would like to go canoeing. They were excited about the idea so we headed for the clubhouse and checked out a canoe and life jackets. As we prepared to launch the canoe I inquired if they had ever been in one before. Looking at each other and shrugging their shoulders, it came as no surprise that they hadn't. Life in the inner-city does not come with canoes.

> **"Problems I can handle. It's the surprises that are dangerous."**

"No problem," I thought. "I'll just hold a short course in canoeing right here on the dock."

I showed the boys how to hold a paddle and how to get into a floating canoe, and I covered the finer points of canoeing in just fifteen minutes. Then after donning their life jackets, Gerry climbed into the front seat and Jean took his position on a seat in the rear. That left the middle of the canoe for me. I struggled to get comfortable as I took my seat on the bottom of the boat. Although the boys were unable to maintain a straight course, we did not do too badly *until the wind began to pick up.*

Those of you who have spent time on a raft or in a canoe know that, after whitewater, wind is the most challenging element nature can throw at you. When the squall came up we were at least a quarter of a mile from the dock. The lake isn't very wide but it is long and deep. Jean, with his limited knowledge and experience, was unable to handle the canoe in a cross-wind, and from my middle position, I was not able to help him. I had to make the decision of toughing it out or trying to change positions with Jean.

Moving around in a canoe at any time is, at best, risky. With the winds and the inexperience of the kids aboard, it was more than I wanted to chance. So maintaining our positions, it took us a full hour to get back to the dock.

As I re-thought the afternoon, I realized that I should never have started out with the boys at each end of the canoe. My place was to command the canoe from the rear seat while allowing the boys to gain experience, from the front. Maybe it hadn't been a life-threatening experience but we certainly could have gotten wet. I had not anticipated the wind and had over-estimated my ability to transfer basic canoeing skills to the boys in a very short time.

Their background was limited and they had never before been on the water. Foolishly, I had tried to move ahead too quickly.

There was probably no harm done, but a wiser me again learned the lesson of looking ahead and preparing for any eventuality. That is what being a father is all about. We need to be in the command position from where we can steer our children safely through the rocks and rough water of growing up.

Our granddaughter Jessi is thirteen; she is very bright, personable, and great with her younger cousins. She has repeatedly expressed the desire to be a doctor. Unfortunately, as she enters high school she will begin to lay the foundation for her grade point average and curriculum content. If she does not begin with top grades in math and science, by the end of her sophomore year a career in medicine might be unobtainable. It does not seem fair but that's the way it is. At thirteen, Jessi already needs to start looking to the future and making preparations if she wants her dream to come true.

In a previous chapter I wrote about Jessi's cousin, Elizabeth, who is a doctor in her first year of residency. Our plans are to have Jessi experience, through a visit with Elizabeth, just what being a doctor is all about. She'll be given the opportunity to decide firsthand if being a doctor is really what she wants to do with her life. The long road begins with high school. Whether she chooses a career in medicine or not is up to her. Jessi's parents and team members just want her to be able to look ahead and make that decision for herself.

Our daughter Lisa did not have an easy time in high school. She made decent grades but success came from long hours of study. When she graduated, going to college was not in her plans. She had had her fill of school.

Lisa was quite satisfied with her career as a nurse's aide in a local hospital. While there is certainly nothing wrong with working as an aide, living comfortably at home, and driving one of the family cars, I was certain that she had not looked ahead at what she would be able to afford on her salary when she was ready to establish her own household.

Biding our time and biting our tongues, Rita and I allowed Lisa the freedom to find out a few things for herself. Almost a year went by before she began to realize that life after high school was not all she had hoped it would be. Lisa had always wanted to become a registered nurse, but after high school she was not at all sure she could make the grade. Finally, she decided to look around for a higher skilled position in the medical field and hit upon becoming a doctor's aide. A local trade school offered a one-year course along those lines, so she decided to check it out. I offered to visit the school with her and as we reviewed the curriculum and walked the facility it became clear that the so-called training was not going to amount to much.

As we left, I asked Lisa what she thought of the school and her career prospects as a doctor's aide. Although I knew that she was quite aware of the school's short comings she remained committed to going there.

After discussing the situation with Rita, I decided to help her understand what living with her decision would be like. One evening we sat down and worked up a budget. If Lisa was really to be on her own she would need an apartment, furniture, and a car. We built the budget around what a doctor's aide would make. Then we hit the road. First on our agenda was looking for an apartment she could afford.

As we drove through likely neighborhoods, Lisa didn't say much, but I could tell from the look on her face that she had been hoping for something a little better than the places that were available to someone on her budget.

Our next stop was a car dealership. We began by looking at the used cars in the front rows—you know, those late models with low mileage. However, when the salesman found out just how much Lisa could put down and pay monthly, he pointed to the back of the lot where the junkers were parked and walked away.

We didn't say much on the way home, and Lisa was quiet for the next few days. Then about a week later she came to her mother and me and said that if it was all right with us, she would like to enter the nursing program at a local college. Two years later she graduated, passed her state boards, and continues to practice her profession as a registered nurse today.

Shortly after Lisa's graduation, I received the following letter:

> Dear Dad,
>
> I've been wanting to write you a thank you note since my graduation and I just feel that this is a good time.
>
> I guess I really want to say thanks for the encouragement you have always given me. You always believed in me and that helped to lift me over some of the lowest points in school.
>
> Dad, I truly believe that if you hadn't given me that push, even though it made me mad, I never would have gone to school. For that, I will always be grateful. You know, a girl I worked with three years ago found out that I just finished nursing school and said, "I bet your Dad was so proud." Then she said, "Lisa, I know that if it hadn't been for him, you would still be an aide." And she's right...

The letter continues with some mushy-love-stuff from a daughter to her father. I won't subject you to that, but isn't it worth all the planning and effort it takes to guide our kids along the correct path for their lives?

Lisa ends the above letter by crediting me with an extraordinary amount of wisdom. In a way, she's right. Fathers are supposed to have more experience than their children. Isn't that why God made parents first?

I think that one of the special talents of men is being able to judge the quality of other men. When hiring employees for the bank I always looked for people with high values as well as proven professional performance. It usually did not take long to recognize the caliber of a man. The way they walked and dressed, the firmness of their handshake, and their ability to look me in the eye all helped me to make my assessment. I was wrong a time or two, but not very often.

As our three girls approached dating age, Rita and I had the opportunity to attend an excellent seminar which dealt with the parent-teen relationship. The host emphasized that fathers are God's protectors for their children, especially their daughters. After the seminar, Rita and I became convinced that I should begin to spend half an hour or so getting to know (size-up) each first-time date as he came to pick up one of our daughters.

I can still remember the family meeting at which Rita relayed our decision. Laura, who was sixteen at the time and the only one old enough to date, began to cry. She stared wild-eyed at us and said, "You mean Dad's going to interview my dates!" I took a deep breath and replied, "Yes, Laura, in a way, yes."

Laura wailed that she would never have another date and that she and her sisters would all be old maids. What boy would subject himself to an interview, she wanted to know. It was a long, painful evening, but Rita and I held fast.

A short time later Laura hesitantly approached me with my first interview opportunity. A young man from her Bible study had asked her out for that Friday night. Although I had thought through how I would handle the interview, I'm sure I was just as nervous as the young man.

He arrived on time. His name was Keven. He was nice looking and well dressed. He had passed the first test.

We sat on the blue chairs in our living room as I began with the usual small talk and chatted about school, family, career plans, and sports, and then I got to the real purpose of our talk. I told him that Rita and I were pleased to have him as our daughter's escort that night. And then I related to him that Laura was the apple of my eye, a special gift from God to her mother and me. I went on to explain that as the man of the house I was also the protector of everyone in my family. I said, "For instance, if we had a fire in the house this evening, my responsibility would be to make sure that all the other family members were safe. I would be the last one out, even if it meant giving up my own life. That's what a father's role is all about."

As we concluded our talk, I told Keven that I would like to have a man-to-man agreement with him as he dated our daughter. I asked his permission to transfer a portion of my role as protector to him while they were together. I was not asking that he lay down his life for my daughter, but I was suggesting that the two of us agree that they would not engage in any activity or go to any place that might place Laura in either physical or spiritual harm.

Be a father who makes things happen.

I let the gravity of my request sink in and then I asked for his hand on it. Keven did not hesitate. He took my hand and our eyes met in agreement. Two men had agreed to protect someone very special. By the way, several years later, Keven married Laura and became our son.

Over the next several years and scores of interviews, I never had to reject a young man, probably because our daughters took care to bring home only quality material. Nor did a prospective suitor ever fail to respond positively to my request. I noticed that they sat just a little straighter and walked a bit taller because another man had respected them enough to trust them with someone of great value—his own daughter.

Our daughters tell us that although their dates always complained prior to their interview, not one of them ever left our home without feeling privileged to have been allowed to take them out. In fact the girls tell us that their dates not only showed them the highest respect but they believe that the interview kept them from being placed in compromising situations that might otherwise have taken place.

We still have those two blue chairs that graced our living room so many years ago. When our family gets together at our home these days, I notice that our sons-in-law will, from time to time, swap stories about their initial interview. I heartily endorse this process and if you could speak with our girls they also would encourage you to try it. You see, the interview turns an ordinary night out into something special and unique. It shows a young man that your daughter is not just another date but a treasure who needs special care and attention.

The examples I have shared deal, for the most part, with older children. However, preparing our children for life starts at birth. Children need to know what to expect from a doctor visit or that first day at school. They need to know what is expected of them in early relationships with friends and family. Life is an unending series of opportunities for dad to prepare the way.

Be a father who makes things happen. Prepare your children for the adventure of life. You will receive untold dividends on the investment of your time and energy.

Discussion Questions

1. Have you had a surprise or two lately?

2. Are you and your wife meeting regularly to discuss the issues that lie ahead?

3. Do you read the directions or just forge ahead?

4. How are you using your team members to prepare for the future?

5. Are you ready for the teen years—dating, driving, college? When will you begin to prepare?

6. Have you told your daughters about your interviewing plans?

11

Creating a Sense of Destiny

In John 14:12, Jesus makes a bold and almost unbelievable statement when he proclaims: "In all truth I tell you, whosoever believes in me will perform the same works as I do myself, and will perform even greater works." He doesn't qualify the promise by requiring us to be intelligent, gifted, or even worthy. He tells us to just *believe in him.* By so doing he knows that we will begin to believe in ourselves and in the power that he has passed on to all believers, enabling them to perform as he did.

I still find it difficult to fully grasp, much less act upon, the promises in God's Word. If you are like me, problems with self-esteem and identity prevent us from even trying to do the things Jesus did. However, when the significant people in my life affirm me and assure me that the service I'm performing is valuable, then I am encouraged to stretch and take risks that I might otherwise avoid.

Early in my business career I learned that my staff, almost without exception, would perform in line with my expectations. If I believed in them, told them so, and expected them to deliver, I was rarely disappointed. Failure came when they lacked self-confidence or were unable to believe in themselves. My attitude and the degree of my involvement could literally make or break them. Just as my staff needed support and encouragement in order to excel, so do family members, church, and community groups. Everyone needs to be motivated and encouraged on a regular basis.

Not long ago Rita and I attended a church leadership meeting. We were discussing ways of enlarging the church's cadre of volunteers. A lay leader spoke about the power of praise and how we need to say thank you often to those who give of their time and talents. The pastor, speaking more to himself than to the group, asked if saying thank you all the time was really necessary. In other words, if we are all working to spread God's kingdom, isn't it enough that we will some day receive our reward in heaven? Then he went on to say, "Yes, I guess it would make me feel better if my superiors thanked me and told me I was doing a good job."

As I caught the eye of another member of the group we smiled—he didn't really understand, did he? But the pastor must have thought about what was said during that meeting, for the very next Sunday his sermon covered Chapter 25 of Matthew regarding the parable of the talents. There Jesus speaks about entrusting servants with small tasks and when they perform well, entrusting them with larger ones. The master praises his servants with the words, "Well done, good and trustworthy servant." After his sermon, our pastor went on to thank the congregation for their dedication and support, then he turned and thanked the music ministers as well as the ushers and everyone else who came to his mind. A smiling congregation left that morning feeling uplifted and more special than they had in a long time.

> **"In all truth I tell you, whosoever believes in me will perform the same works as I do myself, and will perform even greater works" (Jn 14:12).**

As I'm writing this chapter, Rita and I are taking care of our grandson, Chris, while his parents are skiing. After dinner at a local Chinese restaurant last evening, I shared my so-called fortune cookie with Rita and Chris. It said that I was a person who easily "found fault." I smiled as I handed the small piece of paper to Rita and complacently declared, "Not me!" Rita, like most wives, has the ability to bring her husband back to reality. She rolled her eyes and responded, "John, think again." As we drove home I pondered, Am I really a fault-finder or the encourager I picture myself to be? I concluded that there is still work to be done in this area of my life. My kids and grandchildren need all the pats on the back that I can muster. The world is constantly eating away at their self-esteem and so we must begin, early in their lives, to counteract that erosive influence.

In order to get a better handle on young people, teenagers in particular, I asked the youth director at our church if I could have twenty minutes with his group during one of their meetings. I had two questions I wanted to ask them:

1. Were they right now making a positive impact in their family, church, and school?

2. As they grow and develop into adult Christians, did they expect to be an influence for good in their environments?

Not a single teenager out of the almost forty who were present thought he or she was capable of making a difference either now or in the future. I went on to ask about their definition of success. Several talked about college, good jobs, making lots of money—but most were not sure they could ever be a success by the world's standards. It grieved me that those forty young people were moving into adulthood lacking an understanding of their worth, their purpose, and their destiny.

We need to find ways to motivate our youth. It has been my experience that high expectations saturated with encouragement is one of the most potent esteem-building materials known to mankind. Far too often, however, instead of encouragement we tend to put labels on our children, labels that can handicap them for a lifetime.

At a recent Effective Father Seminar in a suburb of Chicago, a man in his late sixties began to share about the quality time he and his wife had enjoyed during the final months of her life. The hour was late, the weather was bitterly cold, and the men were tired. But as the older gentleman talked, we seemed to sense that he needed to share about the recent death of his wife and their relationship of close to fifty years.

The man's two sons were also attending the seminar and the oldest happened to be sitting next to him. From time to time as he talked, he would offhandedly refer to his firstborn as a "throwaway." He confessed that he and his wife had done a much better job of raising their younger son while making many mistakes with the older one.

Although I was sensitive to the man's pain at the loss of his wife, the term "throwaway" made me cringe. I wonder how often that young man had heard himself referred to in that manner. How could he possibly have been expected to develop normally and have a proper sense of self-worth when referred to as *disposable*?

After the closing prayer, I sat down between the father and his son, put an arm around each of them, and thanked the older man for the loving testimony about his wife. As I got up, I smiled at the younger man as I turned to his father. "I'm sure you didn't really mean to refer to this fine-looking young man as a "throwaway," I said. "I think we both know how special he is in God's eyes."

The young man, who was about thirty, smiled and I wish I could have spent more time with them for I'm sure that much repair work is needed in that relationship. A previous commitment kept the father and his sons from attending the final day of the seminar, and so I'll probably never see them again.

A "throwaway" or a special gift from God?

A dear friend was helping me that weekend. We have known Chuck Neff and his wife, Judy, ever since the '70s when we lived in St. Louis. One of the things Chuck shares on the weekends is how he and his wife had two children, Sarah and Bill, early in their marriage and how they felt satisfied and comfortable that their family was complete. Then something happened during a Marriage Encounter weekend that took their comfortable relationship and rekindled their love, fanning it into a flame. Chuck and Judy both felt that this new-found depth of feeling they had for each other needed to be expressed by having more children. Out of that beautiful love came Ann and Mary. Chuck and Judy have always known that those two children were God's way of blessing their renewed commitment to each other.

As Ann moved from childhood into young-woman hood, Chuck decided to share with her about the beauty of her conception and birth and also about his conviction that God has a very special plan for her life. He told Ann that he wasn't sure exactly where God might use her but that he knew, without a doubt, that her impact, wherever that might be, would be great. Ann recently turned sixteen; she is thinking of possibly entering into the religious life or perhaps becoming a missionary to South America. Her plans are lofty because she is firmly convinced that she is special and that her heavenly Father has a unique plan for her life. She heard it first from her earthly father.

Here we have two young people, one described as a "throwaway," the other as a special gift from God. What if all young people could know how unique and special they are? Do you think the atmosphere in our world might just change for the better? I do.

Chuck's talk with Ann is a beautiful model for us to emulate. Something special like this could be added to the birthday celebrations of children and grandchildren. Along with cake and gifts, a birthday party would be an excellent time for mom and dad to share their memories of a child's birth along with pictures and maybe even a video. That child would certainly feel the joy of being wanted and cherished as the details of his or her birth are unfolded for all to hear.

Rita and I recently had the privilege of participating in the birthday celebration for the seventeen-year-old son of our friends, Larry and Chris Dorman. As the mother cut the cake, she told about her son's birth, beginning with what the weather was like and ending with the names of all who were present to celebrate the miracle of life. The birthday ritual had become a tradition over the years in their family of five children. The kids never tired of hearing the stories, especially the one in which they played the starring role. I'm sure that young man (also named Chris) had heard the details of his birth many times before, yet he was all smiles and seemed to sit a little taller in his chair as his particular story was shared with family and friends.

The world is constantly eating away at their self-esteem.

So what will it be—a "throwaway" or a special gift from God? You, your wife, and your team *will* deliver a message to your child. It can be positive or negative—it's up to you.

Besides positive messages delivered repeatedly, children also need the boost to their self-esteem that comes when they know that they are good at something. It may be a sport, music, or even a hobby. It can deal with academics or pets. It can range from chess to crafts. It really doesn't matter, as long as it's their choice. Encouraging them to develop a skill of their own can go a long way toward building self-confidence.

Angie, our ten-year-old granddaughter, experiences difficulty in reading. The results of a comprehensive battery of tests indicated that though she is quite intelligent she has a problem with the way she processes information. This makes it difficult for her to understand instructions for both homework and tests. She will have to work harder than most and it will probably take her longer to finish classroom assignments.

During the final interview with the professional who administered the tests, Angie was asked, in light of her problems, how she felt about herself. Angie replied that she knew she was not a good reader, and that she was often behind the rest of the class, but she knew that she was a valued member of her family (her own words) and that she is the best gymnast in her class.

Among other things, Angie has two huge assets—her family's love and the fact that she is an accomplished gymnast. She knows she is good at gymnastics, and *that* confidence helps her to tough through the other challenges in her young life. By the way, Angie just qualified for state competition. Grandpa sent flowers.

Every young person can be good at something. Help those entrusted to you to find out where their talents lie. Support them in gaining the skills they need to take pride in their accomplishments. Don't let them settle for a back-row seat when a front-row box has their name on it.

Don't settle for a back-row seat when a front-row box has their name on it.

During our last family gathering, we arranged for six of our grandchildren to take daily horseback riding lessons. Each morning the kids and I had an early breakfast and set out for the stables. I had previously discussed the week with the owner and had mentioned that I was interested in having the children gain a basic knowledge of horsemanship. I wanted them to have fun, but I also wanted to see if any of them had a special interest in riding or a natural skill for the sport.

The instructors took their job seriously. Our grandchildren were taught how to use the proper equipment, how to prepare a horse for riding, how to mount, and how to hold the reins. By the end of the week they looked comfortable and secure in the saddle. They were even able to put on a show for their proud parents on the last day. It was a fun week for all. Ten-year-old Julie, however, appeared to have a natural talent and feel for her horse. While the others had a good time, Julie could possibly have found an area in which she might excel. Who knows—some day we may even see Julie in the circle of competition. The choice is hers.

Our challenge as fathers is to look for and place our children in a variety of activities and situations until a fit is found. It doesn't really matter what it is as long as the child shows a real interest and a willingness to work at it. The development of a particular skill, along with encouragement to keep at it, can go a long way toward making young people feel secure and good about who they are.

Family history is another area to consider as we look for ways to help our kids recognize their identity. When our children entered the teen years they seemed to become fascinated with the history of our family. They wanted to know who their ancestors were, where they came from, and the kind of lives they lived. After all, a big part of knowing who they are comes from understanding their roots.

In our home, Rita has an entire wall devoted to old family photographs. Displayed on it are pictures of great aunts and uncles, cousins, and even grandparents whom our children have never seen in person. When she was sixteen, Rita's father died at the early age of forty-eight. There are several pictures of him—one was taken when he graduated from the eighth grade, another shows him playing the trumpet as a young man in a German "Oompah" band, then there's the beautiful wedding picture of him and Rita's mother, and finally there's the special picture taken shortly before his death in 1953. This was an ancestor whom our children never had the pleasure of knowing, and yet through the pictures and the questions those pictures have generated, the kids now have a fairly comprehensive mental portrait of their maternal grandfather.

Help those entrusted to you to find out where their talents lie.

Pictures, old letters, and other ancestral memorabilia are always of interest to children, young and old. Rita has a huge box filled with those things, and, from time to time, when our children and their children are visiting, she will drag it out. What an enchanting way to spend an evening—delving into the mysteries of your family's past. If you have never spent such an evening with your family, I strongly recommend that you give it a try. Stories spawned from old photographs will become treasure to children and grandchildren alike.

Capturing senior family members and their stories on tape has really become a snap with today's electronics. Rita's mother, Evelyn, was much loved by our children. She is gone now, but Grandma Evie can still be shared with the next generation because years ago, to celebrate her seventy-fifth birthday, we asked family and friends each write her a love letter. At her party we recorded the letters as they were read aloud by each author. It was a precious time of sharing, love, laughter, and tears, a time that money could never buy. Our grandchildren, her great-grandchildren, who never had the opportunity to know Grandma Evie personally, can now know her through the eyes of those who knew her best. Evie was a woman of modest means but she had the highest of standards. She was a humble lady who lived her faith and set only the best example for her children and their children to follow.

If you have loved ones who are getting along in years, why not get them to put their story on tape for future generations or, better yet, make a video. No one can tell their story like they can, so seize the moment while there is still time. A family's history needs to be shared even if all the events are not as pleasant as we might like them to be.

"Well done, good and trustworthy servant."

When it comes to passing on heritage and tradition, I believe our Jewish brothers have it all over the rest of us. We live in a neighborhood that is about half Jewish and half Gentile. From time to time, one of our friends will share about a pending Bar or Bat Mitzvah, which takes place when a Jewish boy reaches the age of thirteen or a girl the age of twelve. That is when they are deemed ready to accept the religious responsibility of a Jewish adult. The process has always intrigued me. Why couldn't Christian fathers and grandfathers implement this idea and use that coming-of-age time of life as an occasion to pass on important truths about the Christian faith to our own young people?

When our oldest grandson, Joshua, was approaching the teen years, I thought about having the two of us spend several days of quality time together. After discussing this with Rita and checking with his parents, I set about deciding what I would like to convey during that time. First, I wanted to share my life with him and what history I knew of my side of the family. Second, I wanted him to know what God means to me and how I had arrived at my beliefs. Third, I wanted to discuss what it is to be a Christian man. Thus the idea for the "Christian Bar Mitzvah" was conceived.

During the summer of 1994, we had scheduled a family gathering in the Lake Tahoe area, where our son, Kevin, and his family were living at the time. We had rented a large house next door to Kevin's, and Joshua and I arrived a few days before the rest of the family for our private time together. Our plans were to spend each morning in prayer, study, and discussion while leaving the afternoons free to enjoy the mountains and lakes of the area.

We arrived at our destination late in the evening and decided to get an early start the next morning. After breakfast we sat by the fireplace in the den with our Bibles, books, and papers spread out on the coffee table. About 9:30 there came a knock at the door. A young woman, about thirty, said she was there to clean the house. She said the owners had expected us to arrive later that day and so she was surprised to find that we had already settled in. We told her we would have no problem with her working around us and so she cleaned while we continued our labor of love. I devoted that first morning to sharing my walk with God and my thoughts on how a Christian man is expected to act and treat others.

At times a certain stillness came over the house and I sensed that the cleaning woman was listening to our conversation. When Josh and I were about finished, the woman said she was ready to leave. As she opened the door she turned to us and said she hoped she hadn't disturbed us. Then with tears in her eyes she went on to say that she couldn't help but overhear what we were talking about and that it had been a wonderful morning for her. Her only regret was that no one had ever thought to do the same for her.

Josh and I spent the next three days on family history and discussed gems from the Book of Proverbs and William Bennett's *Book of Virtues* (Simon and Schuster, 1993). But probably most important was the time I spent sharing why I am a follower of Jesus Christ.

It was a powerful three days that I strongly recommend to every father and grandfather. You don't have to fly to some exotic place.

Most important was the time I spent sharing why I am a follower of Jesus Christ.

The sharing can be done right in your own front room or in the local park over peanut butter sandwiches. The value comes as you share your life and your faith, firsthand, with your children or grandchildren. The wisdom you impart may one day be used as a measuring stick for their own life. It may even create a sense of destiny for those who will eventually come after.

I can't admonish you enough, therefore, to make long-term investments in the lives of your children. Be an encourager, help them find an area in which they can excel, put them in touch with their past (family history), and don't be timid about sharing your faith. Such investments are sure to pay hefty dividends as your children tackle the challenges of life and seek to find that special plan God has reserved just for them. It's a splendid burden, but with God's help all things are possible.

Discussion Questions

1. Are you a fault-finder or an encourager?

2. When was the last time you praised your children or grandchildren?

3. What was your first reaction to their latest report card?

4. Are your children mindful that they are a treasured member of their family?

5. Are you aware of the areas in which your children have special skills? Have you helped them to excel in those areas?

6. Have you taken time to share your family history?

7. Where is that old picture album?

8. Have you thought about making a special plan for that next birthday celebration?

9. If you haven't already shared your faith with the children, when will you?

10. Make plans now to hold your own "Christian Bar/Bat Mitzvah."

12

There Comes
a Time...

Some time ago, I heard this story about Vladamir Horowitz. Horowitz was giving an afternoon recital to a packed house in the Boston area. A mother, with high expectations for her five-year-old son just learning piano, felt that listening to the master might be an inspiration to him.

As Horowitz completed the first half of the recital, the audience was entranced. During the intermission the crowd reluctantly moved to the vestibule for refreshments and conversation. The mother, with son in tow, joined friends for a soft drink as they excitedly discussed the performance. Then at the sound of the gong, the audience slowly made their way back to their seats. That was when the boy's mother noticed that he was nowhere to be found. Being a proper Bostonian, however, she endeavored to remain calm as her eyes frantically searched the crowd for her little boy.

As the second gong hurried the throng back to their seats, the boy's mother was still unable to locate him. Thinking that he may have reentered the hall on his own, she made her way back to their seats, looking up and down the aisles as she went.

Just then, the house lights dimmed and as the mother turned, she saw her son—on stage—perched precariously on the bench of the Steinway grand piano. His little hands reached for the keys as a murmur went through the audience and a halting "Twinkle, Twinkle, Little Star" filled the auditorium. As the little boy played and replayed the simple tune, his mother was paralyzed with fear and embarrassment wondering how Horowitz would react to this invasion of his domain.

She was about to make her way onto the stage when Horowitz entered and gently raised his hand motioning her to stop. Then he quietly approached the child from the rear, and as the little boy continued to play his "Twinkle,

Twinkle Little Star." Horowitz reached around him, first with his left hand then with his right, and without drowning out the melody he started to enhance it. There they were, the eighty-year-old master and the five-year-old novice, making beautiful music together and enjoying the moment. The crowd was enthralled, the mother was absolutely delighted, and that little boy experienced a time he would cherish for the rest of his life.

The process we're after is correction.

I see that same type of encounter played out time and time again between father and child. At five, children need lots of help to turn a simple melody into the music of life, but as they gain experience and wisdom, they will be able to carry more of the orchestration by themselves. We, as fathers and grandfathers, are called to gradually use a lighter hand. Then finally, with much practice, our children are able to handle life's composition on their own.

When our grandson Chris was about four-and-a-half, he started learning to ride a bike with training wheels. When he was ready, he and his dad went to a schoolyard, and the training wheels came off. Training time was over. The main event was about to begin.

Chris' dad ran alongside his son. At first he kept his hand on the bicycle seat, then, when he felt comfortable that Chris was in control, he took his hand away but was ready to jump back in, if needed. Finally, the time came when dad stepped back and watched his son weave around the school yard. The bike was not yet steady, and dad held his breath. Then Chris made his first successful stop. Smiling he turned to his dad and gave him a "thumbs up" indicating that everything was okay. From then on, Chris rode his bike on his own. He had taken another step toward manhood.

Rita and I once stayed with Chris while his mom and dad went skiing. It was my job to get him up for school. One morning, I startled him, and he let out a loud cry. As he got up I asked him if anything was the matter. Chris said that he had been having a bad dream. Chris said that in the dream he was helping a friend who was being tormented by a bigger kid. He said that the bully then turned on him and was chasing him as he woke up. Knowing that our grandson has had run-ins with bullies in the past, I asked Chris if anyone was bothering him now. He answered, "No." I asked Chris if he would like to hear a story about when grandpa had a run-in with a bully, and, of course, he was all ears.

When I was about seven or eight years old, a ten-year-old boy lived across the hall from us. He was a head taller and a lot stronger than I was. He would harass me on the way to and from school, when I was at play, or even running errands for my mother. He beat me up whenever he felt like it. I was so afraid that I did not want to leave our apartment.

Chris listened intently. I told him how my stepfather sat me down one day and told me that the only way to stop a bully was to stand up to him. "Oh sure," I thought, "if I stood up to him he would only knock me down again." Then Dad took out a silver dollar and placed it on top of the piano. He said that the dollar was mine the first time I stood up to that bully. A silver dollar in the 1940s was a lot of money. I pondered the situation for a day or two and finally came up with a plan. Since Dana was bigger, I needed some kind of equalizer. I chose one of my roller skates—the old metal kind with a strap.

There comes a time when our kids must make it on their own.

The very next day, armed with my trusty skate, I ventured outside. Sure enough, there was Dana, standing across the street. As he saw me his face lit up. Menacingly he crossed the street until he was right in my face. Then he began to threaten and shove me. But this time it was different; he failed to see the skate I held securely behind my back.

Finally, I got up the courage and hauled off and let him have it. It wasn't a very Christian thing to do, but it did my little heart good to see that bully run home crying and screaming that I had broken his nose. I went right home and got my silver dollar off the piano. Dana's nose wasn't really broken, but from that day on he let me alone.

The story delighted Chris. I cautioned him that a skate might not be a proper weapon because it could inflict serious injury (I guess it depends on how big the bully is, though). But everyone has the right to protect himself or herself, and the thing about bullies is that they will only let you alone once you stand up to them. It is up to Chris' dad, and maybe even his grandpa, to prepare him to face such situations as they arise. He will always have our love and support, but there will be challenges throughout his whole life that he alone will have to confront.

Whether it's school, homework, sports, relationships, or that first job, there comes a time when our kids must make it on their own. Our job is to get them ready to stand on their own two feet while at the same time helping them to understand that they are never truly alone. They can count on their heavenly Father to be with them at all times. In his Word he promises that he will never leave us or forsake us.

As children learn that they must begin to do things on their own, there will be times when they will not choose the acceptable path. They will choose to do things their way, and *their way* conflicts with family principles.

Earlier we discussed setting standards and when a child violates that standard there has to be a consequence. Proverbs 2:6 tells us, "Instruct a child in the way he should go and when he grows old he will not leave it." When I first read that proverb, I thought, "That's just great for when he grows *old*, but what about *now*?"

Words like *punishment* or *discipline* could perhaps be used in connection with the violation of family rules, but I believe the word that best describes the process we're after is *correction*. To correct means to alert, to lead straight, to adjust to some standard, to punish with a view to reforming or improving.

Correction is the process by which a child is brought back to standard by changing his or her behavior. A peaceful home depends upon how everybody understands and obeys the rules. Rules are formed by what the family decides is right and proper. Rita and I took the Ten Commandments (Exodus 20) and worked them into a set of Ream Family Values. Here they are for your review.

Ream Family Values

1. We will place no other gods before the one, true God, Father, Son, and Holy Spirit.

2. We will always respect those in authority.

3. We will respect the person and property of others.

4. We will be truthful, never lying, and always accept responsibility for our actions.

5. We will be honest, never cheating or stealing from God, others, or ourselves.

6. We will be obedient *first* and perhaps question later.

7. We will enjoy each other as a family and have fun together.

8. We will never intentionally hurt another person.

9. We will dedicate ourselves to the service of God, family, and those in need.

10. We will strive to be, and to do, the best we can to fulfill this service.

There is nothing complicated about this list, which we drew up nearly eighteen years ago. For older children it covers just about every area of life. Today there are numerous models for family laws and constitutions—some quite involved. We chose simplicity. We didn't believe that we could improve on God's basic ten.

"Remember who you are."

By the time our children started driving and dating, our rules were so ingrained in them that as they left the house the only thing we would say to them is, "Remember who you are." They knew exactly what we meant.

Once the rules have been laid out and everyone understands them, what happens if and when they are broken? Let's keep in mind that a behavior or course change is what we're after. To inflict pain or take away privileges for the sake of paying a child back for breaking the rules is not consistent with what we are trying to do. Our purpose is to move them back into harmony with God and family.

The initial step in changing behavior is to give a warning—a signal that the child is heading in the wrong direction. Let them know that their behavior is unacceptable and that if it isn't changed they will pay a consequence.

When I first took on managerial duties and was forced to fire people, they were often surprised and did not understand why I took the course of action that I did. I came to understand that a warning along with an outline to correct the situation was a needed first step. When I faithfully followed that process, one of two things happened: Either the problem was corrected and no further action was needed, or the situation became more serious. However, in both cases the individuals knew exactly where they stood.

Corrective action is the next step after an unheeded warning. You and your wife should be in complete agreement about such action. That may not be as easy as it sounds because you come from different backgrounds. If it's a challenge, so be it. Take the time to work it through.

Whether your plan calls for grounding, loss of privileges, extra chores, or even more serious measures, be sure the correction fits both the person and the offense. How grave was the transgression? Was it due to forgetfulness, an error in judgment, or was it rebellion? Rebellion is when a person deliberately breaks a rule or acts counter to family values. It is an act of defiance and disregard for what the family stands for.

Disrespect for authority is one of the most common areas of rebellion. Our friends, the Neffs, deal with disrespect this way. When a child rebels against Judy's authority, Chuck tells the young person that he does not allow anyone to mistreat his wife. The conflict then is no longer between child and mother, it now is between child and husband. Chuck, while protecting his wife from disrespect, is also upholding her authority. Rebellion in any form calls for serious corrective action.

I try to deal with correction issues in a timely fashion, but I also endeavor to wait until my emotions are under control. When I don't wait, I make mistakes. Correction sessions should always be private. The child deserves a hearing and the opportunity to explain his/her actions and express remorse. Sometimes I have changed my mind after hearing the child's side of the story.

Once a correction has been set and explained, however, you and your wife must remain steadfast in your decision. It must be carried out no matter how painful it is for the offender or for the rest of the family. After it is set you must stand your ground. Therefore, be sure you have all the facts and then think through the consequences of the corrective action.

Finally, be sure to cover your actions with love. It's okay to hate the sin, but we must always love the sinner, just as God loves us. There have been times when the actions of our children have been contrary to all we stand for. Although we could not approve of what they did, we never stopped loving them.

Here is a short summary on making corrections:

- Corrections are made to *change behavior* and *return to standard.*

- Correction is a *team effort*. When you and your wife have agreed on an action, you must remain steadfast.

- A correction should *fit the offense and the person.*

- It should always be done *in private.*

- Move in a timely fashion but *never in anger* and always with an *attitude of love and forgiveness.*

Sometimes in spite of all your best efforts, one of your children may stray. We must remember that as parents, it is our job to point our kids in the right direction. They, however, have the choice of either following our lead or choosing a different course. Unfortunately, there will be those who will choose a disastrous road. However, a rebellious child must not be allowed to upset or negatively influence other members of the family—especially the younger children. You must decide whether or not the child will be allowed to remain at home. It is a difficult decision and one that must be prayerfully made.

We once lived up the street from a couple I'll call Betty and Joe. We became very good friends with them. When their son, Bob, was sixteen years old,

Betty and Joe found out that the boy had been using drugs. Despite the parents' efforts, Bob openly defied their authority and refused help of any kind.

The final straw came when Betty found out her son was not only using but also selling drugs. After talking with Joe, they told their son that he could either seek help or move out. He moved out.

One morning soon after, our brand new Oldsmobile was stolen. (We were in the habit of keeping the keys in the visor.) After we reported the theft, Rita called Betty and Joe for prayer. Joe hadn't left for work yet, and he was almost certain that Bob had taken the car. Bob knew where we kept the keys. Although Joe took the morning off and scoured the neighborhood, he was unable to locate either Bob or the car. The police, however, did locate the vehicle and chased the driver into a dead-end street where he abandoned it and fled on foot. The driver's description fit Bob.

A rebellious child must not be allowed to upset other members of the family.

That evening the four of us, Betty, Joe, Rita, and I, sat in our living room while Joe laid out a plan he and I had developed earlier in the afternoon. We intended to use the theft of the automobile to get Bob into treatment. Either he got the help he needed, or I would press charges.

When Betty heard the plan she was beside herself. What if he didn't opt for treatment? Our answer was, "Then he's going to jail." Better that he be in jail than on the streets where he could hurt himself and others. Reluctantly Betty agreed, and I took off for Bob's workplace at the local mall. When I arrived, he was on his break and I located him at a nearby café. Bob was seated in a rear booth and had his head down on the table. Without saying a word I slipped into the seat across from him and pushed a quarter and a small piece of paper toward him. He looked up with his blood-shot eyes and slowly shook his head. I was the last person in the world he wanted to see.

I said, "Bob, you took my car, didn't you?" He looked at me for a long moment and then shook his head yes. Continuing, I said, "Bob, I love you so much that I can't take the chance of you hurting either yourself or anyone else. Here's a quarter and the phone number of the treatment center. You have thirty seconds to make up your mind—either make the call and go in for an evaluation tomorrow or you're going to jail tonight. Your parents and I would rather have you in jail than out on the streets."

Bob looked at me and knew I meant every word I said. It was treatment or jail. Slowly he got up and made his way to a pay phone outside. He kept that appointment and entered the six-week program. Those six weeks were pure hell, not just for him but for his whole family. It was worth it, though. He exited the center clean and dry and continued his rehabilitation with the maintenance program they suggested.

Bob went on to finish high school, then college, where he obtained a degree in chemistry. After graduation he joined the mortgage sales department of my bank. He was one of the top ten sales people for several years running. Bob now is part-owner of his own successful mortgage banking company. He is also married and has two beautiful children.

My favorite part of this story, though, was the day Bob walked up to our house and found me raking leaves in the backyard. He came over to me, gave me a hug and said, "Thanks, Big John. It's been two years today, and I'm still clean and dry."

Be careful. Don't act in haste; seek God's will in prayer. *There comes a time* when tough love is the only answer. But that kind of love often brings the greatest rewards.

Discussion Questions

1. Are you and your wife guiding your children toward independence?

2. Who does the homework at your house, the children or the parents?

3. Will you allow them to fail to learn a lesson?

4. When their allowance is spent, do you give them a handout?

5. Do you have a set of family values, laws, or a family constitution? If not, when will you begin to write one?

6. Are warnings part of your parenting process?

7. Does your family have a correction process? Do you follow it each and every time it is needed?

8. Could you ask your older teenager to leave your home if the rebellion was serious?

13

Cover Them with Love

Cody Jennings was the daughter of friends of ours in Atlanta. This brave little girl died of cystic fibrosis in 1980. Following is the sermon that was given at her funeral Mass.

I am comforted that so many of you have come this morning. Perhaps you sense, as I do, that God has been doing something very quietly in our midst. What we do here this morning is not something that touches only the Jennings family; it touches all of us. I thank you all for coming.

To help me with this sermon this morning, the Jennings family have shared with me their recollections of Cody's last hours. She was in considerable pain, found it hard to breathe and hard to talk. Yet, at the very end, she insisted on drawing one more picture of Jesus as the Good Shepherd to give to her family. Her thoughts at the end were of others. She thanked her mother and father for having been so good to her. She was glad they would not need to worry any more about her missing school. Would someone please tell her pets that she had died so they would know? She wished her father a happy birthday and said she wouldn't be able to come to his party. She said she wanted to be buried in Atlanta near the family, and was troubled about her two little brothers who were buried in Oklahoma [they had also died of cystic fibrosis].

When her grandparents called from Oklahoma she took off the oxygen mask and spoke very strongly to them because she knew Grandpa was hard of hearing. She told them she was dying and that she loved them. She knew she was near death and had no fear of it.

She asked Jesus to come for her.

The Jennings family obviously feel that Cody was very special. I think we all agree.

What I think I am supposed to say today is that the Jennings family is very special. I only have a glimpse into this, but I believe that when God sends someone special like Cody into this world, he chooses very carefully where he will put the special someone.

The birth of Jesus is a case in point. He is very special. And when Jesus came, he came to a couple who had been chosen very carefully. God prepared Mary very specially to be the mother of his son. And yet Joseph and Mary never prospered in the way other families of their day prospered. God's special ones fare rather badly, it seems, by any other standards than God's.

At the very end Cody said, mysteriously, "My mission is accomplished." What could she possibly have meant? What on earth would lead this thirteen-year-old to think that she had a mission, and what would encourage her to think she had accomplished it?

As my mind went over and over these words, I came to believe that I understood what she meant. I think Cody's mission in life was to be loved. She was dropped into the midst of the Jennings family to be loved. She was dropped into *our* midst to be loved.

All of us are dropped into this life to be loved. This is almost a definition of who we are—someone special looking to be loved. As if God fashioned us very specially and lovingly and then placed us down carefully in the world, and then looked around expectantly at everybody as if to say "Love this little one."

Brian and Terry, and all of the Jennings children, you are, each of you, someone special, looking to be loved.

Can you see me as someone special, *looking* to be loved, *needing* to be loved, *hoping* to be loved? Can you hear each person in this room asking, "Who will love me?" If you can, can you hear all of us calling out, "We will!"

Perhaps Cody would say, "Well, I have to tell you, I can't do much. I've got cystic fibrosis." And we would say, "All the more reason to love you. We love you, Cody."

Someone else might say, quietly, "I'm an alcoholic." And we would say, "We love you just as you are." And others would give their own reasons why no one should love them. I'm divorced. I'm gay. I can't find work. And someone would be sure to say, "I don't think I belong in this group." And we would say, "Oh, yes you do. If you think you don't belong with us that means you really do belong here." And we would gather round him and give him a hug.

Finally, we understand. Cody is each one of us. And her mission was to teach us by her life in her family who we are and what God asks of us. That we must love one another.

Yes, I agree, Cody came to show us that each and every one needs to be loved. From the highest level executive right down to the newest tiny baby, we are created to be loved and to love. Jesus gave us that new commandment in John 13:34-35: "Love one another; you must love one another just as I have loved you. It is by your love for one another, that everyone will recognize you as my disciples."

If nothing else in this book has hit home with you, my prayer is that you can grasp Jesus' command to love. We do not have a choice about whether or not to love our children. It is a direct command. As fathers we are to cover those entrusted to our care with repeated acts of love. I will be more than satisfied if my children and grandchildren will remember me as a lover. I may have made tons of mistakes, but I pray that they will never doubt my deep and lasting love for them.

The woman who cuts my hair and I often talk about family. One day, when I was writing this chapter on love, I asked her, "From the time you were a little girl and on through your teen years, were you sure your father loved you? And if so, how did he communicate that love to you?"

After pausing for almost a minute, she said, "Yes, he loved me, but we didn't get along when I was a teen. He's much better with our children than he was with me." I offered that maybe, since his grandchildren aren't his direct responsibility, he feels free to just relax and enjoy them. Then I asked if he ever said, "I love you, Rachel," and if he was a touching dad. She was reluctant to reply but the answer was clear. No, he wasn't much on telling or touching. She had to figure out how he felt on her own.

Is Rachel's experience exceptional? No; my encounters with numerous individuals tell me that it is really very common. The vast majority of us men make our loved ones guess how we feel. Why is it so difficult for us to express our feelings? Could it be the heritage passed down to us from thoughtless or even abusive fathers? Whatever the reason, it is just not good enough. God commands us to love one another—not in silence or from afar but in a personal, intimate way. His model for us is the relationship between the Father and the Son. In Mark 1:11, the Father tells his son, Jesus, at his baptism, "You are my son, the beloved, my favour rests on you." Other translations use, "You are my son, whom I love, with you I am well pleased" (NIV). The Modern Language Bible says, "...in thee I am delighted." The Living Bible says,

"...you are my delight." What a powerful message of encouragement to the Son or to any son or daughter if they could hear similar words from their own dads.

Neither my natural father nor my step-father ever said those words to me. But I can break that chain of silence in my own family. I can give my children and grandchildren the time and attention they need so that they will never doubt how much I love and delight in them.

I once spent an afternoon babysitting my two-year-old grandson and three-year-old granddaughter. We ate cookies and milk, played "Raptor" (dinosaur), and read about insects. At one point, I found that I just could not delay a trip to the bathroom any longer. After making sure that all the doors were locked and that all knives and other dangerous implements were out of reach, I made my visit. Almost immediately, the children began banging on the bathroom door and calling for Grandpa. I assured them over and over again that I would be out in just a moment, but nothing seemed to work. They wanted Grandpa *out now*!

Have they heard you say "I love you?" Do they understand that you are well pleased with them?

All at once a deep silence fell over the house, and I became more than a bit concerned. A quiet two- and three-year-old can mean big trouble. Then I spied a tiny hand, fingers first, coming under the bathroom door. With the fingers wiggling, a tiny voice called, "Grandpa, are you still in there?" Since shouts and banging hadn't worked, now they were going to try hand signals! I couldn't help but laugh at the lengths our little ones will go to to seek the attention of their mothers, dads, grandmas, and grandpas. They desperately need us and will do most anything to gain that attention, that assurance that they are loved.

Have you taken your loved ones in your arms and told them how much they mean to you lately? Have they heard you say "I love you?" Do they understand that you are *well pleased* with them? If you haven't done these things, when will you?

Why allow another week, or even a day, to go by with the slightest doubt in their minds? Give your children and grandchildren the example they need to enter into their own love relationships (marriage and children) whole and confident that they are, and always have been, loved.

Jesus' baptism has yet another message for us. In Matthew 3:17 this scene is handled from a different perspective. As John baptizes Jesus, the heavens open and the Father says, "This is my son, the beloved, my favour rests on him." The Father here is speaking to the crowd watching from the shore. He publicly acknowledges his love for Jesus and that his Son is treasured and of great worth.

Not only is it important to share our love one-on-one with our children but we are to profess that love and affirm our kids in public. Graduations, recitals, sport events, birthdays, and other family gatherings present excellent opportunities for us to acknowledge them.

I remember the wedding of the son of one of our dearest friends. At the rehearsal dinner, the father of the groom told intimate, endearing stories about his son. The father's voice was filled with love and pride as he reminisced. The bride's sister later told my friend how moved she had been by his loving tribute.

Don't be timid about being openly affectionate. Imitate God the Father and share it with the crowd. Nothing does more to build a child's self-esteem than looking at himself through the loving eyes of his father.

> **Don't be timid about being openly affectionate. Imitate God the Father and share it with the crowd.**

It is important, though, that our words are backed up by our actions. If you tell your children that their activities are important to you and yet you can never find the time to show up, your words are hollow. Actions always speak louder than words.

Words spoken in private and in public, along with actions that back them up, are a large part of the love equation. Facial expressions, however, can also convey the way we feel about someone. For example, a new father's face conveys the overwhelming love and pride he has as he holds his child for the first time. "You are mine," he's thinking. "I helped to make you out of my love for your mother. We'll be always together. We'll go fishing, my son, and I'll teach you to play ball." Or "How beautiful you are, my daughter. You remind me of your mother. I can't wait to see you in a frilly little dress with pretty ribbons in your hair."

Our looks can show approval or disapproval. Looks of unconditional love are a fantastic way to show that we mean it when we say, "I love you."

Finally, touching is also an important way to communicate love. Shaking hands conveys an amiable attitude. We show friendship with an embrace. A kiss says, "I love you and want to be with you." An affectionate touch tells our children not only that they are loved but that everything is okay. They have our approval.

We are created to be loved and to love.

An interviewer once told me he was concerned about touching his teenage daughter. He said, "You know, with all this talk about sexual abuse, I'm afraid she'll get the wrong idea." Although I tried to be polite I thought, "If you had established a loving trust in your relationship with your daughter as she was growing up, you wouldn't be concerned that she might misinterpret your touch now." I have always hugged my kids, kissed them on the cheek, or squeezed their arm as a way of saying, "I love you." There is nothing wrong with an appropriate touch that, for a brief moment, connects you to the one you love and reinforces that love relationship.

There may come a time when a son will become uncomfortable with hugs and kisses. That's okay. Abide by his wishes, but talk about it. Tell him you'd like to have a signal, just between the two of you, that says, "I love you." It could be an arm around his shoulder, a pat on the back, or a squeeze of his arm. Whatever you agree upon is fine. Touching is a natural way to be close to those we love. It has been proven that babies need to be touched to thrive. They do not develop normally without loving attention.

Covering our children with love when they are lovable is one thing, but how should I react when my children are unlovable? We have to remember that love is more than a feeling; it is a decision. From time to time we are all unlovable. Rita and I would never have made it through the past forty years together if we had totally relied on our feelings.

Loving relationships with our teenage and young adult children can often be difficult. The questions of morals, values, and lifestyles come up often. Once again let me suggest that we must love the sinner but reject the sin. One of my favorite Gospel passages is Luke 15:11-32. It's the story of the Forgiving Father—better known as the Prodigal Son. I'm sure you are as familiar with the story as I am. The younger son leaves the family, breaks with God's laws, squanders his inheritance, and then comes crawling back begging for forgiveness and to be allowed to return.

The father is overjoyed and runs to meet his son, ordering rings for his fingers and the fatted calf for a celebration. This infuriates the older son, and his father answers him with, "My son, you are with me always and all I have is yours. But it was only right that we should celebrate and rejoice, because your brother here was dead and has come to life; he was lost and is found" (Lk 15:31-32).

He could only have been found because Dad kept the door open for his son's return. No matter what they do, no matter how much you have been hurt, never, never do or say anything that could permanently close the door. The opportunity for them to repent and return must remain available at all times. We don't have to approve or condone, but we are called to love and to forgive.

Cover your children with *love* both in public and private. Do this through your words and through actions that confirm your words. Do this through your eyes and your touch, through forgiveness, and with a heart and arms that are open wide. Let the Father and his Son, Jesus, be your role model as you become a father of velvet and steel.

Discussion Questions

1. Do your children know you love them? Are you sure?

2. When was the last time you said "I love you" to them— both in private and in public?

3. Have you kept your promise to be there for them?

4. Do your looks and touches reinforce your words?

5. Do you still love even when the kids are unlovable?

6. Are all your doors still open?

14

Don't Try It Alone

I have stressed that you and your children's mother need to make every effort, through dialogue, prayer, and compromise, to work together for their good. You also need a team of helpers to support the two of you. But even then you cannot be truly successful as a Christian father without understanding that God—Father, Son, and Holy Spirit—is to be the head, the guiding influence, of both you and your team. But is this true? Let's do a little self-examination.

First let's deal with the Father. Can you express what God means to you? Can you share with your children why you believe in a loving, all-powerful, Father God who created them and who has a unique plan for their life?

Second, do you believe that Jesus Christ, the Son of God, is Savior and Lord? Do you understand that he came not only to save but to heal? Can you believe in his promises?

> John 1:12: "But to those who did accept him he gave power to become children of God, to those who believed in his name."
>
> John 3:16: "For this is how God loved the world: he gave his only Son, so that everyone who believes in him may not perish but may have eternal life."
>
> John 14:6: "I am the Way; I am Truth and Life. No one can come to the Father except through me."
>
> John 14:12-13: "In all truth I tell you, whoever believes in me will perform the same works as I do myself, and will perform even greater works, because I am going to the Father. Whatever you ask for in my name I will do."

Mark 16:17-18: "These are the signs that will be associated with believers: in my name they will…lay hands on the sick, who will recover."

John 14:16-17: "I shall ask the Father, and he will give you another Paraclete [advocate] to be with you forever, the Spirit of truth."

Third, who is this advocate, this Holy Spirit, that Jesus talks about in John 14? Do you understand that when Jesus left this earth he sent the Holy Spirit to be here with us? It is the Spirit who enables us to *do the same things Jesus did and even greater things*. Have you encountered the Holy Spirit? Are you familiar with the way he works in power and in truth? If you haven't encountered him personally, how can you? Jesus tells us in Matthew 7:7-8: "Ask, and it will be given to you; search, and you will find; knock, and the door will be opened to you. Everyone who asks, receives; everyone who searches, finds; everyone who knocks, will have the door opened."

You may not be able to answer all these questions right now, but you do have Jesus' promise that if you *seek* you will *find*.

Just as Rita and I cannot understand one another unless we engage in ongoing communication, I cannot expect to understand the ways of the Lord unless I dialogue with him on a regular basis. By dialogue I mean talk to him; have a quiet time set apart for just the two of you, listen as he speaks to your heart, and not only read the Scriptures, but pray them. Seek and you will find, he said. It's a promise.

When you begin to establish that ongoing communication with God, good things begin to happen. As your relationship grows you will come to understand what he would have you do in various situations. Difficult relationships becomes easier to handle. The path to honesty, integrity, and purity becomes clearer. Accepting the unlovable traits in those around you is now possible. Gradually you are becoming wise and mature in his ways. Time apart with God is never time wasted.

Developing a personal relationship with God is an ongoing journey. It doesn't happen overnight, on a weekend, or at a retreat. It can begin there, but any long-term friendship takes time, trust, communication, and eventually, intimacy, to mature. A short poem written by Rita describes this journey.

Gradually We Become

To grow in Christ is a gradual thing,
It doesn't happen overnight,
How much we have to look forward to
When we keep the Lord in our sight.

Each day as I read His Word,
It becomes just a little bit clearer.
And each day, the Lord to me,
Becomes just a little bit dearer.

We understand that good relationships require time, trust, and communication, but what does it mean to be intimate with the Lord?

Some years ago I was asked to speak at a retreat about developing a "personal relationship" with Jesus Christ. Although everyone there was familiar with that term, I was searching for a more graphic way to illustrate that intimate, loving relationship.

It was a beautiful spring day in St. Louis. The sun, bright and warm on the April flowers, announced that winter was over. Signs of new life were all around us. During a break, Rita and I took a short stroll along a path that overlooked the Mississippi. As we walked, I became fascinated with the interaction going on between a couple walking ahead of us. The husband and wife walked slowly, hand-in-hand. As they moved they brushed together gently. He whispered something in her ear and she laughed. He then placed his arm about her waist as they walked down a short flight of steps. They were enjoying the day, but more importantly, they were enjoying each other. The two were in harmony, walking in step, heading in the same direction, and at peace with each other and the world around them.

I smiled and thanked the Lord. He had just given me the example I needed for my talk. That was the portrait of a close, personal relationship with him that he wanted me to convey. God gave me this picture in the form of a husband and wife, but it could very well have been a father and son, or even you and Jesus. Jesus wants to walk hand-in-hand with us each day. He wants to share our innermost secrets and desires. He wants us to feel his arm of protection and guidance at all times. But most of all he just wants us to enjoy him and rest secure in the knowledge that he always has everything under control. All we need to do is make the choice to invite him into our lives.

"Okay," you say, "I've opened the door and invited Jesus into my life. Now what?" How do you go about cultivating that friendship? The answer isn't difficult. Learn about him (read his Word), communicate with him (pray and listen), and make his friends your friends (Christian community).

Over the centuries thousands of books have been written about God, but as far as I know, he has only authored one—the Bible. Learn as much as you can about your Friend by delving into his Book. The four Gospels are a good place to begin because they tell us about Jesus' life on earth. My favorite happens to be the book of John; you might start there. Or take a look at Proverbs—it is full of wisdom. Psalms can put a song in your heart, and Acts tells how the early Christians survived as a community with the aid of the Holy Spirit.

The Bible is not only a collection of writings, however. Hebrews 4:12 says, "The word of God is something alive and active." This means that not only am I able to learn about God, but he can speak to me through the pages of Scripture in every circumstance of my life.

Both the Old and New Testaments are filled with hundreds of stories, parables, truths, and teachings that are as authentic and applicable today as they were when they were written. Make the decision now to get into God's Word. It is the best book for fathers that has ever been written. Read a

Search, and you will find.

little Scripture before going to bed at night. It will clear your head of the day's distractions and help you get a good night's sleep. Or perhaps you could get up thirty minutes early each morning and spend that time getting to know the Lord through the pages of his Book.

If you don't have thirty minutes, don't let that stop you. You can take a single verse, like John 10:10 for instance, and contemplate it throughout the day—"I have come so that they might have life and have it to the full." My concept of a full life has changed over the years. I once thought that being a Christian would cramp my style. How could I have a good time, be a success in business, have lots of friends, and still be a Christian?

But I do enjoy a full life filled with friends of the highest caliber, and I count myself successful beyond my mother's wildest dreams. Jesus came so that you and I might have life and have it to the full.

Now that you are coming to know your Lord through his Word, it's natural for you to want to talk with Jesus. Communication is the next step in developing your relationship with him.

While I'm comfortable with traditional prayers, my personal choice is dialogue. I chat with the Lord all day long—in the shower, taking a walk, driving the car, riding my bike. Wherever I am I know he's there too—a part of my day and a part of my life. I want to be the man he wants me to be. I'm praying to him as I write these words.

Although I treasure daily dialogues while I'm out and about, I find that it is in the quiet times, those times set apart just to be in his presence, that I am most able to listen and understand what he is speaking to my heart. It was Samuel who said, "Speak Lord, your servant is listening."

Sharing prayer with those you love is another great way of enriching your relationship with God. My wife and I spend time each morning remembering our family and friends in prayer. We acknowledge the Lord as the head of our house and the third person in the trinity of our marriage. We also spend time just praising him for who he is and thanking him for all he has done for us. As a father, don't miss the opportunity to pray with your children before a test, at meals, at bedtime, or when they are sick. Cover them with your love and protection. That's what being a Christian father is all about.

"As for me and my house, we shall serve the Lord." (Jos 24:15)

We've talked about getting to know Jesus through Scripture and dialogue. Now it's time to meet his friends. If you are not part of an alive church community, find one! The advice Rita and I give our children is to seek out a church and observe its people. Are they there because they want to be or because they think it's their duty? Before we would move into a new area, Rita and I would visit the local churches and have a nice long talk with the pastors. We chose a church that would not only nourish us spiritually but also afford us the opportunity to serve. Find a church that meets your needs as it encourages you to grow. Find one where the preaching is alive and deals with the problems of everyday life and gives Gospel answers. In that kind of atmosphere you will find people who love the Lord—people you will want to call friends.

I hope that the church you choose has an active men's ministry, preferably one in which men with common needs meet weekly in small groups to seek God's answers to life's problems. Fathers and grandfathers, in particular, need the kind of support this type of ministry provides. "Iron is sharpened by iron, one person is sharpened by contact with another" (Pr 27:17). If there aren't any small groups available, then take the initiative and form one yourself. Begin by carefully choosing the friends with whom you would like to share, find a convenient time, get to know one another, not just socially but spiritually, and then just share your week. If there are problems, pray about them. If you have an answer that worked for you in a similar situation, share it. Make it clear that everything that is shared must stay within the confines of your group. Over time, your love and trust for one another will bloom and grow into friendships that may last a lifetime. You have nothing to lose and everything to gain. Start making your plans today. Just do it!

Please don't try to walk the path of fatherhood alone. You won't make it. Each of us needs that personal relationship with Jesus Christ in order to gain the wisdom, knowledge, and understanding we need to oversee our families.

So get to know Jesus, talk and listen to him, and surround yourself and your family with his friends. I know of no better way you can prepare to become the most effective velvet-and-steel father you can be.

Chapters 24 and 25 of Joshua tell the story of the prophet's last years. As leader of the Israelites, he has gathered the tribes before him. He reminds them of all that Yahweh has bestowed upon them. How Yahweh protected them in battle, helped them defeat their enemies, and guided them to the Promised Land. He goes on to say that they now have begun to waver, to move away from and to lose sight of God. Joshua then asks, "What will it be, men? Will you worship and follow the heathen gods, or will you return to Yahweh our God?" He turns to them and answers his own question. "But as for me and my house, we shall serve the Lord" (Jos 24:15, KJV).

My prayer is that every man who reads this book will be able to answer as Joshua did. "As for me and my house, we shall serve the Lord."

Discussion Questions

1. Who or what do you believe in?

2. Are you prepared to share your faith with your children? If not, when will you be?

3. Do your children see you at prayer and reading your Bible?

4. Are you praying with your children? It isn't difficult—give it a try.

5. Is your church an active Christian community?

6. Do you have any close male friends? What are you waiting for?

7. Whom will you and your family follow?

Resources For Men

MEN ARE NO DAMN GOOD (Pending Further Research)
Essays on Becoming a Man
Eugene J. Webb, Illustrator: C.P. Houston
Paper, 192 pages, 5½" x 8½", ISBN: 0-89390-343-4

What is it with men anyway? Guys need to laugh at themselves, brag about themselves, and cry about themselves _ and have a good time doing it. So these witty essays about becoming a man are just a pleasure. Any helpful insights and unnerving pieces of wisdom are totally accidental.

BALANCING YOUR LIFE
Setting Personal Goals
Paul Stevens
Paper, 96 pages, 4¼" x 7", ISBN: 0-89390-375-2

The key to improving your life, according to noted _worklife" expert Paul Stevens, is planning. All you need is privacy, peace and quiet, a pad of paper, and lots of enthusiasm. *Balancing Your Life: Setting Personal Goals* provides that extra push. It will help you sort through the conflicting issues you deal with each day, the opportunities you want to explore, and the actions you need to take to bring balance to your life. In the end, you'll emerge with a set of clear personal goals that will put you in charge of your dreams.

WHEN YOU ARE THE PARTNER OF A RAPE OR INCEST SURVIVOR
A Workbook for You
Robert Barry Levine
Paper, 104 pages, 6" x 9", ISBN: 0-89390-329-9

The partners of rape or incest victims are also victims. As a partner of a rape- or incest-survivor, you may feel that you too, must keep your pain, suffering and anger a secret. This workbook benefits survivors because its approach is sensitive to many of the key issues survivors face in their healing process. It also teaches you, the partner, how to be supportive to the survivor's needs, while becoming aware of and dealing with your own needs and concerns.

RISING ABOVE
A Guide to Overcoming Obstacles and Finding Happiness
Jerry Wilde, PhD
Paper, 144 pages, 5½" x 8½", ISBN: 0-89390-345-0

This book, by a psychologist who had to face his own life-threatening disease, lays out some tools that will help you face any dilemma with a minimum of suffering. Great referral book for counselors.

Call Toll-Free 1-888-273-7782 for current prices.

See last page for ordering information.